BLEEDING HEARTS...
BLEEDING COUNTRY

Bleeding Hearts...
Bleeding Country

Canada and the Quebec Crisis

DENIS SMITH

M. G. HURTIG LTD.-PUBLISHERS-EDMONTON

M. G. Hurtig Ltd., Publishers
10411 Jasper Avenue
Edmonton, Alberta

ISBN 0-88830-048-4

Printed and bound in Canada

For Dawn

Contents

Acknowledgments

I am grateful to a number of colleagues for their critical comments and advice. David Cameron and William F. W. Neville read the complete manuscript in draft; W. L. Morton, Stuart Robson and Donald V. Smiley read individual chapters. Their perceptions have done much to refine my understanding of the Quebec crisis and its implications; but the point of view and the imperfections of the argument remain my own. The manuscript was typed under the pressure of a deadline by Mrs. Arlene Davis, to whom I am also grateful.

Champlain College,
Trent University,
April 30, 1971.

Introduction

Although there had been some disturbing intrusions upon the calm of Canadian life before October, 1970, most English-speaking Canadians still managed, more or less, to keep the forces of modern history at bay. History, on the whole, was something that happened elsewhere but not at home, while Canada quietly pursued its destiny of liberal progress. This had not been a realistic assessment of the country's situation for decades; but in many ways Canada had remained sufficiently insulated from the disruptive social forces of the twentieth century to allow the complacent self-image to remain.

One result was that our institutions and our theories of politics could be taken for granted. We had inherited our political beliefs, our language of politics and our institutions from other sources and, after an interlude of creative adaptation in the 1860s, we could fairly safely leave the thinking to others. The talents of Canadian politicians seemed to be the very practical talents of brokers, mediating the material and cultural interests of developing communities spread across a continent. The politicians did not seem to require the aid of philosophy, nor even to understand what such aid might mean. We were all philosophic liberals, and there was no chink in that armour of optimism through which analysis could penetrate.

In the last sixty years the liberal world built out of the nineteenth-century imagination has been in disintegration. But in a modern world which had ceased to work, Canada appeared still to work pretty well. When the shocks finally began to come, they were severe and we were unprepared for them. We did not know, in the first place, how to perceive our emerging situation as a minor economic satellite of an imperial United States. And that meant we did not know what to do about it. (George Grant, Walter Gordon and the Waffle group began to give us the means of locating ourselves in that relationship.) We did not know, in the second place, how to perceive our association with the French-speaking community in Quebec, once that community threw off its spirit of submission after 1960. For ten years Quebec writers and politicians told us we had to confront the question; we responded with a mixture of puzzlement, goodwill, indifference, and occasional hostility. But we did not think much about what was involved, because our liberalism taught us, *a priori*, that the federal system was the best political work of man. It was a work of reason, it was infinitely flexible, and it had sufficed for a hundred years. It would surely meet the challenge.

In 1968, perhaps to silence any doubts that troubled us about Quebec's satisfaction with Confederation, we enthusiastically endorsed a French-speaking prime minister who promised to maintain the federal union and to refuse Quebec any kind of special status. That election effectively suppressed the beginnings of debate in English Canada about the renovation of Canadian federalism, and in practice it made the system inflexible. The discussion of constitutional change that followed occurred on Ottawa's intransigent terms, and it was sterile. By the autumn of 1970 the discussion had reached a dead end, but Ottawa continued to reassure the country that matters were sorting themselves out. Only Quebec seemed frustrated by the impasse—which did not worry the rest of the country because it scarcely knew what Quebec thought anyway. Our politicians and journalists could offer little enlightenment. The federal cabinet, too, became the complacent victim of its own propaganda.

In the spring of 1970, two plots by the terrorist Front de Libération du Québec to kidnap diplomats in Montreal were discovered and broken by the police. In September, reporters in Montreal repeated warnings from the Front that further kidnapping attempts were imminent. The governments of Quebec and Canada gave no public hint of anxiety at the threats (which may have been understandable), but they also apparently took no special police precautions to forestall the possibility. When the first political kidnapping came on October 5, 1970, the governments and the public were taken by surprise. They were even less prepared for the second kidnapping six days later.

The broad course of events that followed is well known: after ten days of futile political manoeuvring, the army was called into Quebec. The next day the federal government proclaimed the War Measures Act, outlawed the FLQ and granted special powers of search, arrest and detention to the police in the province. One day later Pierre Laporte was murdered by the FLQ. Five hundred persons were detained by the police over the next few weeks, and almost 450 of these were released without charge. Bail was eventually granted to all but two of the remaining detainees. (These two, Pierre Vallières and Charles Gagnon, were, in effect, held in preventive detention without conviction as they had been for months after their previous arrest in 1966.)* The emergency police sweep failed to locate the two terrorist cells, but normal police activity did so after several weeks. In December one cell, when discovered, negotiated the release of its hostage in return for the suspension of criminal charges against the kidnappers and the provision of safe passage to Cuba for themselves and members of their families (an offer previously made by the governments). Later that month, the remaining fugitives from the other cell were discovered, and surrendered after a period of negotiation. They were charged with kidnapping and murder.

A temporary emergency measures Act was adopted by Parliament in December, 1970, to replace the powers exercised

---

*Following his acquittal on a charge of seditious conspiracy, Gagnon was finally released from prison on bail on June 16, 1971, pending an appeal on a contempt of court conviction and trial on a charge of membership in the FLQ. Vallières' bail application on June 23, 1971, was uncontested by the Crown and he, too, was released while awaiting trial on a number of charges.

under the War Measures Act, and this temporary act was allowed to lapse on April 30, 1971. At this point the Front de Libération du Québec ceased to be a banned organization (although several dozen persons remained to be tried after April 30 on charges arising out of War Measures and the successor Act).

The terrorist deeds and the use of emergency powers preoccupied the country in the months after October. Very basic questions were raised about the real course of events, the responsibility for those events, the propriety and prudence of suspending civil liberties, and the motives of all the actors engaged in the drama. Federal ministers, journalists, and many citizens participated in the discussion: the affair shocked and disturbed the country, perhaps more than any other event in its history since 1867.

But a great difficulty of comprehension remains. Canadians do not regard themselves as a brutal people, and as a result the events of October possess the exceptional quality of nightmare. The public cannot quite believe what happened, nor understand why. But without that understanding its judgment is impaired. This book is an attempt to examine some moral questions raised by the events, to place the events in a broad political framework for the sake of greater enlightenment, and to consider, finally, what choices Canada and Quebec should make in future, in the light of a radically altered pattern of political forces. It is one effort, among many that are now required, to think our way through the Canadian crisis. I believe that a major shift of perspective is necessary if we are to cope with the consequences of October, 1970, in a way that will preserve our liberty and our democratic tradition. I am not at all confident that the shift can be made.

The book makes clear that I was an opponent of the response to terror chosen by the governments of Canada and Quebec. I remain an opponent, on grounds which will, I hope, become evident. What is important to me now is that we should not compound the errors of 1970 and fall deeper into political folly.

1:   A human life

"It is a difficult decision when you have to weigh a man's life in the balance, but our commitment to society is greater than anything else. We cannot let a minority group impose its will on society by violence."[1] These were the first public words of Prime Minister Pierre Trudeau on the substance of the ransom demands made by the Front de Libération du Québec following the kidnapping of James Cross, the British trade commissioner in Montreal, on October 5, 1970; and notwithstanding ten days of open communication with his kidnappers in the Front de Libération du Québec, they remained the definitive general statement of federal policy in the crisis. While the Hon. Mitchell Sharp had said in the House of Commons on the day of the kidnapping that "the Canadian government . . . is fully aware of its responsibility for the protection of foreign representatives in this country and is sparing no effort to discharge this duty,"[2] the prime minister's statement defined the limits of Canada's effort to save the life of Mr. Cross. There would be an intensive attempt by the police to find and release him; there might be some speculative probing of the intentions of the FLQ in the hope either of assuring that its murder threat was a bluff or of breaking its will; but there could not, according to the prime minister, be any question of a major concession to terrorist demands. That would be to "let a minority group impose its will on society by violence." Having put the alternatives this way, Mr. Trudeau made clear that his "difficult decision" would in the end be to permit the sacrifice of a man's life if necessary, because "our commitment to society is greater than anything else."

Mr. Sharp elaborated the federal government's position slightly in the House of Commons on October 6, when he told the House of the seven demands made by the kidnappers:

> The communiqué demands that these conditions be met within forty-eight hours from the time of the issuing of the communiqué. Clearly, these are wholly unreasonable demands and their authors could not have expected them to be accepted. I need hardly say that this set of demands will not be met. I continue, however, to hope that some basis can be found for Mr. Cross's safe return. Indeed, I hope the abductors will find a way to establish communication to achieve this. All the authorities concerned are dealing with this case on the basis that we have the double responsibility to do our best to safeguard Mr. Cross and at the same time to preserve the rule of law in our country.[3]

At the minimum, this declaration sought to buy time. Perhaps at that point, only a day and a half after the abduction, this was a reasonable wish on the part of the federal government. The kidnapping had obviously come as a surprise, and a prudent response might reasonably take more than one day to be worked out. Above all, such a response would require a delicate judgment of the FLQ's determination; this was dependent upon police intelligence and perhaps also upon some overt sign from the kidnappers. Implicit in Mr. Sharp's statement was a hint to the FLQ that some substitute set of demands might prove acceptable to the government. Whether this hint was meant seriously is unclear, but the omens were not hopeful. From the outset each side had shown itself sufficiently intransigent that a face-saving compromise seemed unlikely. So the agonizing game began.

It was later reliably reported that Mr. Sharp's statement to the House reflected a firm decision taken that day by the cabinet committee on priorities and planning:

The basic decision was not to follow the example of Latin American and other governments which had faced similar terrorist demands and decided to comply. Trudeau and his ministers were united in deciding not to release the terrorists already in jail.

But they also decided that they must try to keep Cross alive while gaining time for police investigation, and the agreed tactic was to pretend to offer to negotiate.[4]

Such a decision had ominous consequences which may not have been entirely foreseen by a government that was psychologically unprepared for the crisis.

If the FLQ really was bluffing, and was unprepared to commit murder, no great danger could be involved in playing for time. But if that judgment entered into Ottawa's initial response, it was surely naive.[5] As members of the cabinet later said in seeking to justify the imposition of War Measures, the FLQ had given abundant public evidence of its fanaticism and determination in seven years of bombings, thefts and killings; and the intensive efforts of a combined antiterrorist squad had repeatedly failed to extinguish the organization or its variants. Kidnapping and assassination had been boldly advertised by spokesmen for the FLQ as the next stage of revolutionary activity.[6] The group's propagandists had excused and applauded the use of violence in their writings and speeches. The record of political kidnappings in other countries since 1968 indicated the complete seriousness of the threat; the game was not one to be entered lightly. And even if there had been evidence of bluff (which there had not been), is it tolerable for a democratic government to take risks with a man's life on that assumption?

Three of the seven demands made by the FLQ cell holding Mr. Cross were couched in the bravado style of guerrilla theatre: the requests for reemployment by the federal government of four hundred and fifty mail truck drivers, for delivery of $500,000 in gold bullion, and for public disclosure of the identity of an alleged police informer. The experience of political kidnappings elsewhere, and a straightforward judgment of the terrorist psychology, suggest that these were mere propagandist

exercises which only the most delirious terrorists could expect
to be met. They could safely be ignored. The kidnappers in fact
soon made clear that failure to meet them would not lead to
the murder of Mr. Cross.[7] The fundamental demands (on
which any deal to release the hostage would rest) were for the
publication of the FLQ manifesto, the release of twenty-three
persons convicted of or charged with terrorist offences, and
provision of safe passage for these persons and their families to
Algeria or Cuba. Against these basic demands, the federal government on its side opposed three abstract commitments: to
"the rule of law," "to society," and against dealing with blackmailers. These expressions became the shorthand, almost cod-
ed, justifications for the refusal of Ottawa and Quebec City to
meet the FLQ demands. Until the televised statement of Jerome Choquette, the Quebec minister of justice, minutes before
the last deadline set by the FLQ cell, and six days after James
Cross's abduction, no public explanation of the meaning of
these commitments was attempted by any minister, federal or
provincial. Some press commentary in this period, however,
suggested that a trade of convicted prisoners for the hostage
would give the FLQ a major propaganda victory, increase its
confidence and daring, undermine the authority and self-confidence of the state, invite further kidnappings followed by even
higher ransom demands, and so on down the slippery slope to
chaos.[8]

The subsequent rationalizations for the use of War Measures suggest that this kind of reasoning stood behind the official commitment to social order and the rule of law; but one
cannot be sure how articulate the reaction was. In a civilized
society, there is a habitual distaste for the methods of violence
which is instinctive and emotional rather than reasoned, and
there can be little doubt that shock and disbelief played a large
part in the official reaction to the FLQ's initiative. "The picture which emerges, of the first few days of the crisis," wrote
Anthony Westell, "is frankly conceded by participants to be of
a government in shock, almost in trauma."[9] The absence of any
full attempt by Canadian political leaders to justify their acts in
that first week offers some evidence that the stance of the au-

thorities was not a reasoned one based upon any careful calculation of alternatives. Not to consider the alternatives, however, suggests a curious indifference to the value of an individual life, an inability to apply humane imagination to a potentially tragic situation. How much was one life worth? Were the possible consequences of a "hard line" really any easier to estimate, more certain, and less risky than those of a compromise with the FLQ? The case for the relatively unyielding position finally taken by the Trudeau and Bourassa governments on Saturday, October 10, rests upon the view that a rejection of compromise was unquestionably the most prudent course. But the evidence for that case has been taken for granted rather than presented satisfactorily by the Trudeau and Bourassa governments. It is less than overwhelming.

One decision apparently taken by Ottawa and Quebec during the first week of the crisis was to play down their concern in public. Prime Minister Trudeau delegated the role of spokesman for the federal government on the affair to the secretary of state for External Affairs, Mr. Sharp, rather than assuming public leadership himself. Ottawa conspicuously refused to be diverted by the kidnapping, and pointedly carried on its public business as though nothing unusual had occurred. On Thursday, October 8, the speech from the throne opening the new session of Parliament spoke with unprecedented complacency about the political good fortune of Canadians.[10] The prime minister's office reasserted Mr. Trudeau's intention of departing as planned for a state visit to the Soviet Union in the following week. Prime Minister Bourassa of Quebec determined to carry through his scheduled visit to New York in pursuit of increased American capital investment, leaving his minister of justice, Jerome Choquette, to manage the provincial side of the liaison with Ottawa.[11] Apart from covering Mr. Sharp's few appearances during the week, reporters in Ottawa fell back upon discussing the ostentatious creation of an 'Operations Centre' for the crisis in the East Block, which seemed intended to reassure Canadians that all the instruments of the electronic age were being relentlessly applied to resolution of the affair. This technological emphasis reinforced the impres-

sion (whether intended or not) that human emotions were not
deeply engaged in the matter, and that political competence
could be equated with technological efficiency.[12] But technology without policy is hollow; the curiosity of the press led its
speculations beyond this façade, to the question of who was
determining policy, and especially to what role Prime Minister
Trudeau was playing in the affair.[13] Premier Bourassa, away in
New York City, appeared to be, by choice, a long way in the
background.

The prudence of this low-keyed response to the kidnapping,
like the prudence of playing for time, depended upon a gamble
that the abduction could be satisfactorily dealt with in a few
days by the police. If Mr. Cross had been safely rescued, and
the kidnappers arrested, within a few days, Mr. Trudeau and
Mr. Bourassa would have reaped political credit for refusing to
exaggerate the seriousness of the incident, and for remaining
calm under extraordinary pressure. But the case was not broken by the police, and by Wednesday evening the provocative
defiance and self-confidence shown by the FLQ in its communiqués had palpably begun to rattle the governments. At that
point, a fundamental reassessment of official policy was desirable. The time for preliminary judgment had passed; now that
the seriousness and skill of the cell had been demonstrated
clearly, it was vital to consider quickly whether *any* of the
demands should be met, and if so, which ones; whether any
substantial alternative offer should be made in the hope of
freeing Mr. Cross; and whether the prime minister of Canada
or the prime minister of Quebec should come forward out of
the shadows to explain and justify their policy to a public
which was also beginning to grow uneasy.

The first consideration which demanded such decisiveness
was that of the safety and morale of Mr. Cross and the feelings
of his family. If the governments did seriously intend to protect
his life, the establishment of a negotiating position which offered a reasonable chance of being accepted by the kidnappers
had become urgent. Their deadlines were passing, and as far as
anyone outside the FLQ cell knew, every further attempt at
delay involved a cruel risk to Mr. Cross's life. A second and

increasingly important consideration was the effect on public
sentiment of an extended display of cliffhanging by the authorities. The longer the affair dragged on indecisively, in full suspense, and without any formal public statement of reassurance
by Mr. Trudeau or Mr. Bourassa, the more distracted and
confused the public was bound to become.

But if a general reassessment of government policy toward
the kidnapping took place at this point (and there is no evidence whatever that it did), it did not result in a clearcut
decision to save Mr. Cross's life by meeting the minimum terms
of his abductors. Rather, the policy of firmness was softened
slightly, with the effect of gaining further time. Mr. Sharp indicated on television that the federal government would be willing to permit Radio Canada to broadcast the text of the FLQ
manifesto, and on Thursday evening, October 8, this was
done.[14] This first concession, however, did undermine the previous pledge of the federal government not to bargain with
blackmailers. Mr. Sharp had in fact entered the bargaining
process, and had done so on national television. The effect was
probably threefold: a public prepared for firmness by the previous statements of Mr. Trudeau and Mr. Sharp had its assurance unsettled; the element of the public favouring compromise
was offered its first encouragement; and the kidnappers were
given some reason to expect that continued defiance on their
part would more and more weaken the government's resolve.
The agreement to broadcast amounted to evidence that the
FLQ was winning the battle of nerves, but not that Ottawa was
yet prepared to yield decisively.[15]

Two days of uncertainty then followed the broadcasting of
the manifesto on Thursday evening. The timing of the ultimate
government statement on Mr. Cross, delivered at 5.30 P.M. on
Saturday afternoon, October 10 (just one-half hour before the
final deadline announced by the FLQ in its seventh communiqué) indicated either that the details of the two governments'
definitive response to the kidnappers had not yet been worked
out by Wednesday or Thursday, when the original concession
was made, or that the primary concern of the authorities was
only to play for time. As late as Friday afternoon, October 9,

Jerome Choquette gave evidence of temporizing by appealing to the kidnappers to provide proof that Mr. Cross was still alive and in good health.

The disturbing effect of Mr. Choquette's statement on Saturday afternoon could hardly have been greater. For six days, the Canadian public had been kept on tenterhooks while the kidnappers and the two governments exchanged demands and counter statements over national radio and television. The Front de Libération du Québec, with extreme propagandist skill, established the rules of the game in this period by demonstrating that no direct communication between the parties would be acceptable, despite Mr. Sharp's invitation to communicate privately. The whole country was swept along in the drama. Ottawa and Quebec City found themselves pulled willy-nilly into the public arena, and fumbled through these days of tension at the mercy of the FLQ, as one after another of the deadlines proclaimed by the kidnappers was reached and passed with maximum publicity. The Canadian Broadcasting Corporation, contributing its macabre judgment to the heady situation, prefaced Mr. Choquette's televised address on October 10 with a telephoto shot of the parliamentary Peace Tower clock approaching the FLQ's deadline of six o'clock, and concluded the special broadcast with the same picture as the clock ominously tolled the hour.

The situation was agonizing and unprecedented for those who had to meet it, and one can sympathize with any politician who must face such events; but the unfortunate course of the affair suggests that the way chosen by the Trudeau and Bourassa governments was, apart from total capitulation, the least prudent among the remaining alternatives.

Given the original statements of Mr. Trudeau and Mr. Sharp, which were notable for their toughness, the consistent and decisive act would have been to refuse all communication with the kidnappers, to concede nothing, and to establish this position unequivocally by Wednesday or Thursday evening. The potentially tragic result of such a choice was evident, and the public might reasonably have expected some formal explanation of the stand from the person who, in the end, would be

responsible for taking it: Prime Minister Trudeau. Such a decision, clearly communicated, would have forced the hand of the
FLQ. Either the organization would then indicate its weakness
of will by backing away from its threat, risking a loss of face;
or it would carry out the threat, or another act of terror, with
the ruthlessness it had boasted of. In either case, having been
pushed to its choice quickly by the unrelenting firmness of its
antagonists, the terrorist group would have lost some of its
initiative. If the prime minister had immediately followed such
a decision with an appeal to Parliament and the public for their
confidence, and their support for vigorous police action to
meet the specific threat of the FLQ, he would still more effectively have removed the initiative from the FLQ and calmed
the public before the growth of any general alarm and confusion. These attempts to pre-empt the initiative would also, of
course, have had to be accompanied by swift efforts on the part
of the police to protect hundreds of prominent public figures in
Quebec, the potential targets of further kidnappings.

   This kind of action, taken within three or four days of the
abduction of Mr. Cross, would at least have demonstrated the
resolution of the governments and their determination not to
be panicked or confused by terrorist acts. In the later days of
the crisis, supporters of the two governments (and especially
editorial commentators abroad, who were distant from the details of events) in fact credited the authorities with precisely
this kind of resolution. For a large part of the public, it was
an obvious reassurance to be able to fall back upon that faith
once War Measures had been invoked. There had been, it was
frequently argued, a choice between a hard line and a soft
line; Mr. Trudeau and Mr. Bourassa had stiffened themselves
and chosen the hard line, and the country had been saved
from revolution.

   But this is not what happened. The two governments, rather,
showed themselves to be uncertain and diplomatically inept. If
the headline writers and their audiences ignored the details of
events, the terrorists undoubtedly did not. The governments'
ambiguous response itself contributed fundamentally to transforming an ugly incident into a frantic national crisis.

While a decisive rejection of the terrorist demands, presented in an assertive way, might have taken the initiative from the FLQ, it would also have risked James Cross's life. In contrast, to do the utmost to assure his safety, Ottawa and Quebec had to make a major concession to the terrorists. The sixth note from the cell holding Cross, dated Thursday, October 8, and delivered to a Montreal radio station the next day, said that:

The Front de Libération du Québec suspends temporarily its threat to execute the diplomat J. Cross, following the broadcast of the political manifesto by Radio Canada.

Here are the last two conditions that the ruling authorities must meet to keep diplomat J. Cross alive:

1. Liberation of "consenting" political prisoners and their transportation to Cuba or Algeria, as set out in the first communiqué items 3 and 4.

The wives and children of the political prisoners must be allowed to accompany them if they so desire.

Lawyer Robert Lemieux, Pierre Pascau and Louis Fournier must be allowed to witness these operations and see to it that they are carried out satisfactorily.

2. The immediate suspension of all searches, raids, arrests and tortures on the part of the fascist police forces.

When we decided to abduct the diplomat Cross, we took into consideration all possibilities, including that of the sacrifice of our lives for a cause that we believe to be right.

If police forces happened to discover us and tried to intervene before the British diplomat Cross is released, be sure that we will defend our lives dearly and that J. Cross would be executed at once.

And we are in possession of enough dynamite to feel "safe."

Guarantees:

The Front de Libération du Québec pledges solemnly before the Quebec people to release alive and well the diplomat J. Cross within the twenty-four hours that will follow the return to Montreal of the observers who accompany the political prisoners.

　　These observers must, upon their return, confirm publicly that the operations were completed satisfactorily . . .[16]

A seventh note with the same date announced that:

> This is the last communiqué should the ruling authorities not free the political prisoners between now and 6 o'clock Saturday night. Neither the ruling authorities nor their fascist political police will find the diplomat J. Cross if they do not carry out our demands formulated in communiqué No. 6 in the time limit set above.[17]

These two messages contained crucial keys to the mentality of the cell holding Mr. Cross. First, the murder threat was lifted in response to the government's concession in broadcasting the manifesto: the kidnappers thus demonstrated that they were not intransigent, but were reasonable enough to respond to proposals for compromise. Second, the remaining demands were reduced to the minimum in expectation of a further response to their flexibility by the governments. Third, the cell pledged its word "solemnly before the Quebec people" to carry out its part of the final bargain it had now proposed. Fourth, the cell indicated that its members had effectively dismissed the problem of their own safety, and were willing to risk their lives in the affair.

　　Whatever direction the next step by the authorities was to take, the evidence in these communiqués of the state of mind of the kidnappers should have been heeded if official policy was to be as sensitive to the situation as possible. But the evidence appears to have been ignored. The communiqués suggested that the cell's public reputation for good faith was important to it. Having made its commitment, it would very likely have held to it for the sake of displaying to the public that it possessed a sense of honour, if the release of prisoners had occurred. In any diplomatic negotiation in which some kind of peaceful resolution is desired, it is an elementary rule of prudence for both sides publicly to concede each other's good faith—whatever they may think in private. There could be no pur-

pose any longer in expressing doubt about the reliability of
the FLQ's promises, except as a means of undermining the
chances of agreement and humiliating the cell before its own
constituency.

The renewed statement of the cell's determination offered
evidence that any concessions aimed at the safety of the kidnappers themselves would be inadequate to secure Cross's release. What they desired was not their own security, but the
release of prisoners. When determined men go to the length of
kidnapping for a political cause, the reasonable assumption is
that they have passed the point of concern about their own
lives. If they had not passed it, they would not have committed
the act in the first place.

What Mr. Choquette displayed in his statement of October
10 was not political skill and firmness, but bad judgment and
infirmity of will, applied in such a way that the result turned
out to be defiance of the FLQ. Following a turgid defence of
the established democratic order and the reforming impulses of
his administration, Mr. Choquette did not firmly reject a deal
with the terrorists: instead he made a counter offer. He asked
the kidnappers to "take account of our good faith," to release
Mr. Cross, to accept his pledge that the parole procedure in the
cases of the convicted terrorist prisoners "will be followed
objectively," and that, in the cases of those prisoners still before the courts, "we will consider the cases with clemency, with
a clemency that is opportune in view of your gesture which
should put an end to terrorism here." And finally, he offered
safe conduct out of the country for the kidnappers in return for
giving up their victim.[18]

The logic and moral consistency of the official response was
destroyed by this statement. What careful observer could any
longer credit that original pledge to uphold the rule of law and
to stand firm against terror? The defence of the state's integrity
had become hypocrisy. Mr. Choquette had hinted at some unusual guarantee of "objectivity" in the parole hearings of terrorist prisoners (implying its previous absence); he had promised
to seek clemency in the cases still before the courts; and above
all, he had promised to suspend entirely the application of the

criminal law in the case of the kidnappers themselves. There could hardly have been a more dramatic example of extra-legal diplomatic bargaining; but it was astonishing in its ineptitude. The self-confidence of those who claimed to uphold the authority of the state had been undermined, because the state had revealed its willingness to bend the rule of law under terrorist pressure; but the counter offer fell so far short (in both its psychology and its substance) of what the FLQ required that the release of Mr. Cross at that moment was inconceivable. Despite all their protestations about the sanctity of the rule of law, the governments had limply displayed their own indifference (or confusion) over the principle.

From the public evidence, it is impossible to judge what was the intention of Quebec City and Ottawa in delivering this statement. It did not buy time, it did not display self-confidence, it could not achieve the safety of Mr. Cross. Was it the result of a bad compromise of conflicting attitudes to the kidnapping, or a naive but quite sincere attempt to satisfy the abductors with half-measures, or an effort to rally the majority of the Quebec public behind an official repudiation of the FLQ's demands? Mr. Sharp's explanation to the Toronto *Star* suggested the latter. Whatever the motives behind the statement may have been, the result was to offer a defiant challenge to the FLQ either to capitulate or to demonstrate its fanatic will anew and raise still further the stakes in the crisis. But a challenge to capitulate, when the challenger does not have the power to enforce it, risks ridicule and counter-challenge: it brings on the very deterioration of public authority that it is meant to prevent.

And this is one crucial reason why a bargain for the release of James Cross was desirable. The first reason, of course, was both human and political: life and liberty are worth protection, and a state which claims itself committed to their maintenance is obliged to deliver on that commitment when it faces the choice of doing so. If it fumbles, or refuses the occasion, it acts immorally and throws into confusion the meaning of its belief in the sanctity of life. Mr. Choquette did those things for Canada on October 10. But he also played from a false position of strength, and in doing so revealed the hollowness of his power. He asked for a response from the FLQ which his government and the federal government were in no position to enforce. Seldom does the emperor himself confess that he has no clothes; it is an imprudent act for any authority. But Mr. Choquette left the FLQ with the message that the state was irresolute and powerless to control the situation.

A civilized and free state is always at the mercy of fanatics, as long as it wishes to remain civilized and free. It may take very limited (though necessary) steps to assure efficient policing of the community, but it cannot insulate itself completely against terrorist activity. If terrorism occurs, the fragile web of public order has already been broken, and the state cannot wish the disturbance away. Nor can it afford rashly to disregard its most elementary obligation. When innocent lives are at stake, the best it can do in the immediate situation is to save those lives, and not risk them by pretending to a mastery of events or an ability to predict the future that it does not possess.

To put life first in this kind of crisis is only to reaffirm the standards of decency and humanity we so glibly proclaim in the abstract.[19] It is, in a sense, an act of weakness for the state; but in another sense, it is an act of moral strength, for it demonstrates that life is actually regarded more highly than political 'face.' If terrorists have threatened life, and the state acts successfully to preserve it, the state has reason to argue that it has reinforced its claim to authority, while the terrorists have relinquished theirs. For the state to ignore a life it has the power to save, however, is to descend to the same crude level of *realpolitik* as that occupied by the terrorists. In conditions of war, when violence is used as a matter of course by both sides, such commitment to individual lives is brutally abandoned; but Canada was not in a state of war after October 5, 1970. It was forced to deal with just one kidnapping, and the possibility of others, and in doing so it was still obliged to act from normal civilized standards. Perhaps the two governments were still confusedly trying to do this on October 10. But if so, they seemed unable to sort out their moral and political confusions sufficiently to make a realistic offer for Mr. Cross's safety.

2: "A state of confusion"

The statement by the Quebec minister of justice called forth the predictable response from another FLQ cell. "The government refused to give in," wrote James Eayrs. "Its reward for such holy obstinacy was the kidnapping, minutes after the final deadline passed, of the Quebec minister of labour."[1] The second cell had sprung into frenetic preparation following the abduction of James Cross, and on Saturday afternoon it was ready to act. "We came back . . . and waited for the press conference of Choquette," Bernard Lortie testified at the Laporte inquest. "When we realized that the government was not giving in, the kidnapping was definitely on."[2] Pierre Laporte, minister of labour and manpower, minister of immigration, and House Leader of the Quebec government, the senior colleague of Prime Minister Bourassa, was not under police protection. He was picked up without a struggle in front of his home, and disappeared until the discovery of his body the following Saturday evening. If politicians in Quebec City and Ottawa had been able to treat the first kidnapping with a degree of naive or cavalier detachment, this second coup brought them rudely to alert. Within twenty minutes of the final government declaration on the Cross affair, the FLQ had again stolen the propaganda lead with a kidnapping more reckless and provocative than the first. As the televised tolling of the hour on Parliament Hill had symbolized, the country had been waiting anxiously, fearfully, with a touch of masochistic expectancy, for the next move in the deadly game. The FLQ played brilliantly to that expectancy.

The simple psychology of those who favoured firmness suggested that appeasement of the FLQ would be followed by further kidnappings, and implied on the other hand that resistance to terrorist demands would unquestionably discourage the terrorists. As one federal minister, Otto E. Lang wrote:

> Surely the way to resist blackmail and to save lives and freedom of people in the future is to resist firmly and remove completely the payoff or reward for this kind of activity.[3]

Apart from the mistaken impression that the formal response to the kidnapping of Mr. Cross had actually been one of firm resistance, there is in this argument a substantial claim that cannot be justified. Mr. Lang uses a commercial metaphor to describe the relationship between the government and the terrorists, according to which the terrorists have offered to sell their merchandise for a price. If the customer rejects the bargain, the seller is rebuffed, withdraws his goods from the market, and gives up seeking the same kind of exchange again. If there is no expectation of payoff, there will be no kidnappings.

Judging political kidnapping in such limited terms excludes the possibility of understanding terrorism. Even the metaphor is misapplied: in a free market, if the price is too high, the seller reduces it to permit an agreed exchange. That reading of the kidnappers' position would have borne some closer relation to reality, since they had indicated a willingness to bargain. But "the payoff" for terrorists involves much more than the receipt of ransom; as Prime Minister Trudeau recognized, it involves the achievement of notoriety and semi-legitimacy, a reputation for boldness, organizational skill, determination, the faithful representation of public grievances, and a proven ability to outwit the authorities. It is this broad reputation that governments and citizens committed to nonviolence have to counter. The decision whether, and to what extent, specific demands should be granted must be made within that wider context: and

one should not begin the calculation by assuming that the refusal of demands will necessarily undermine the terrorists' reputation and self-confidence. A government which moves quickly to cut its losses in a kidnapping case by freeing prisoners
may well be acting wisely in this kind of subtle conflict.

Some foreign observers of the Canadian crisis showed less
certainty in their advice to be firm than did Canadian politicians. More than one editorial, like that of *The Economist*,[4]
treated the Canadian case as a kind of laboratory experiment,
in which a hard line was desirable because it had not been
adequately tested elsewhere. As the *Manchester Guardian* admitted tentatively after War Measures had been invoked:

> Mr. Trudeau's cabinet chose the tough way out of the
> blackmail dilemma. It is too early to say whether it will
> work. If the aftermath of the present kidnappings and the
> Canadian government's policy of mass arrests brings a de-
> cline in violent activity by the FLQ it will have succeeded.
> But no one can be sure yet. In Brazil and Uruguay the
> tough and gentle policies have both been tried. Neither has
> been conspicuously successful. But those are countries
> where political violence by government as well as insur-
> gents is deep-seated. That is not the case in Canada.[5]

There was no such admission of fallibility from the two governments or their supporters, nor even, in Ottawa, from members
of the opposition in Parliament. Some sign, among all the
country's elected representatives, of strong doubt about the
wisdom of the official course was surely desirable at this point
as a contribution to the country's critical balance. But among
politicians only René Lévesque, the leader of the independentist Parti Québecois, offered that kind of cautious warning
against dogmatism when he said on October 8 that "I hope
that the people in power as well as the authors of this unjustifiable act will seek above all to avoid a tragic ending."[6]

The Toronto *Globe and Mail* took a similarly discriminating
position in its leading editorial of October 12, following Mr.
Laporte's kidnapping:

The governments' refusal to free the prisoners has been described by some observers as a hard line, a description which implies that a decision to release all or some of them would have been a soft line. Perhaps that has been our greatest error in all this wretched business—to assume that courses open to us are hard or soft. All the courses are hard.

To release the prisoners, to allow them to escape the charges that face them or the penalties that have been imposed on them—to do so with a dagger in our back— is to accept ignominy. To refuse to release them, to accept the forfeit of Mr. Cross's life should the kidnappers carry out their threat, is also ignominious.

Between the two, we would have chosen a deal on the release of at least some of the prisoners. We have a very solemn obligation to protect the representatives of other countries who come to do business in our midst. When we fail to protect them we must be prepared to accept whatever humiliations lie in the way of reasonable rescue . . .

The FLQ now has two hostages and has stated its readiness to seize more. Will our response be any different from that when there was only one? More important, would our response be any different if there were 50 or 100 hostages—perhaps as many as there were on the airstrip at Amman? If it would, then it should have been different when there was only Mr. Cross.[7]

The abduction of Mr. Laporte was dramatic proof that the FLQ did not accept the official theory of its own behaviour. It would not shrink away when its demands were rejected. The second kidnapping should have brought home to the two governments that their defiance did not contribute to the maintenance of the law or to public calm and order, and that they had misinterpreted the assumptions on which the FLQ was acting. But instead, in a curious and irrational way, the governments and their supporters were now inclined to put things backwards to justify official policy. The claim that "firmness" would inhibit further acts of blackmail was maintained in face of the contradictory evidence of Mr. Laporte's kidnapping; the second kidnapping was itself offered as proof that appeasement would not work against such dastardly enemies.[8] This was just the first example of extreme contortion in defence of the official line; it was especially worrying because it indicated panic and the departure of critical reason from the scene.

The kidnapping of Pierre Laporte brought the crisis home as Mr. Cross's had not. For governments accustomed to dealing with events at a distance, the first kidnapping, while crude and unprecedented, did not appear to hit very deeply, because James Cross was a minor foreign diplomat outside the central circle of power and personally unfamiliar to the country's leaders. The Cross abduction offered a better test of the human imagination of the Trudeau and Bourassa governments than did the second, because it was a case to be considered in the abstract, without the moral strains of personal acquaintance with the victim. For that reason, as Paul Rose (the Laporte kidnapping suspect) recognized,[9] it offered a relatively poor political test of the resilience of the two governments in crisis. They could choose to reject the terrorists' challenge in this case without great moral turmoil, and in expectation that the public, too, would take such a decision with general calm. The silence of the federal parliamentary opposition during the first week of the affair, and the calculated restraint of editorial commentary, which were both intended to avoid complicating the two governments' handling of a delicate situation, perhaps unwittingly reinforced the habitual tendency of the governments to act without imagination or utmost urgency after Mr. Cross's disappearance. The decision of October 10 in effect to repudiate the terrorists' minimum demands came relatively easily, or at least without many signs of agonizing debate and self-questioning on the part of ministers in Ottawa and Quebec City.[10] But Mr. Laporte's case was a different matter.

For the government of Robert Bourassa, Mr. Laporte's capture was the most dismaying and complicated challenge it had yet faced, striking to the heart of the cabinet's compassion, self-confidence and self-interest. Pierre Laporte's political experience had been a powerful source of strength in an otherwise young and inexperienced government; he had established his authority as government leader during the first session of the National Assembly under Premier Bourassa in the summer of 1970; he was a moderate nationalist whose participation in the Quiet Revolution had given him respect and support well beyond the Liberal party.[11] He was close to being indispensable; Robert Bourassa spoke of Laporte later as his own "right arm."[12] Laporte, too, had fought Bourassa for the leadership of the party only ten months before, and any demonstrable reluctance on Mr. Bourassa's part to protect the life of his colleague might arouse the cruel suspicion that there was a lingering animosity between the two men.

For the federal government, as well, the kidnapping complicated the crisis. While federal leadership was easily defensible in dealing with the kidnapping of a foreign diplomat, the sensitivities of a provincial government were now directly involved. They could be ignored or overridden only at the peril of creating a major incident in federal-provincial relations. What is more, Pierre Laporte was the personal friend and political associate of the Quebec members of the federal cabinet too; their personal feelings were now also bound to be engaged. (Among other things he had contributed to Pierre Trudeau's and Gérard Pelletier's pioneering political journal of dissent, *Cité Libre*.) The FLQ had forced an extreme test of political adroitness, conscience and nerve upon Ottawa and Quebec City.

Undoubtedly this test unsettled the members of the Quebec cabinet. Premier Bourassa called them into emergency session on Sunday afternoon at his Montreal office in the Hydro-Quebec building; during the day he consulted with Prime Minister Trudeau, the leaders of the three Quebec opposition parties, and at least once with Claude Ryan, editor of *Le Devoir*.[13] The cabinet deliberated under pressure of the FLQ's new 10 P.M. deadline, with a desperate letter from the kidnapped minister before it, in which Mr. Laporte pleaded for the key concession:

You have the power to dispose of my life. If it were only

a question of that, and this sacrifice were to produce good results one could think of it, but we are facing a well-organized escalation which will only end with the release of the "political prisoners." After me, there will be a third one, then a fourth, and a twentieth. If all political men are protected, they will strike elsewhere, in other classes of society. One might as well act now and avoid a bloodbath and a panic indeed unnecessary.[14]

Faced with this plaintive appeal, the two governments once again spun out the preparation of their response until the last possible moment. The only rational explanation for the excruciating delay through the afternoon and into the evening was that no unambiguous reply could be agreed upon. In that case, the most that could be hoped for was some message which would persuade the two cells to extend their time limit once again; and that extension could only be expected if the possibility of an exchange of prisoners was held out more positively than before. But an ambiguous statement designed to satisfy politicians with conflicting views, and yet also to get a deceptive message across to the FLQ, would require the most diplomatic wording. The statement which emerged gave indication of such painful care.

At three minutes to ten, a private Montreal radio station broadcast a short recorded message from Premier Bourassa. Unlike the statement by the justice minister of the previous evening, this one was primarily addressed to the kidnappers rather than to the wider Quebec public. It noted that the FLQ communiqué following the Laporte kidnapping had referred to the original seven demands, but that the letter from Mr. Laporte had spoken only of two requests, to suspend the police search and to exchange prisoners. The premier therefore proceeded to deal only with the essentials, though indirectly:

It is because we particularly want Mr. Laporte and Mr. Cross to live that we decide—before discussing the demands that have been made—to set up mechanisms that would guarantee, as Mr. Laporte says it will, that the re-

lease of political prisoners will surely result in the safe
release of the hostages.

That is a prerequisite that common sense forces us to
require and it is for this reason that we ask the kidnappers
to contact us.

Indeed, how can one accede to the demands without
being convinced that the counterpart will be fulfilled? The
Quebec government believes that it would be irresponsible
toward the state and to Mr. Laporte and Mr. Cross if it
did not insist on this safeguard.

We want to save the lives of Mr. Laporte and Mr.
Cross and it is because we want it with all our strength
that we are making this gesture.[15]

The message's concentration upon mechanisms of guarantee, and the request for communication from the FLQ, led
some commentators (including those of the CBC English-language network) to interpret it as a flat rejection of the FLQ
demands. These concerns, after all, had been expressed already during the previous week. But this message went further, speaking for the first time of the possibility of "the release of the political prisoners," and of the mechanisms as "a
prerequisite" and "a counterpart" to the release of prisoners.
There was no promise that Quebec would accede to the demands; but there was the strongest hint that it would do so if
it could engage in discussions under adequate guarantees of
their successful outcome. The statement was a skillful compo-
sition aimed at encouraging the FLQ to talk, at bringing to
Bourassa's side those who already advocated a negotiated settlement, and at carrying along the political elements opposed
to such a settlement. It was also an assertion of provincial
leadership in the crisis, aimed at avoiding the embarrassments
of any additional federal initiatives. The Ottawa government
was not mentioned in the document.

Once having made this intervention, Mr. Bourassa had to
carry it through to completion if he wished to maintain his
authority as prime minister of Quebec. A squeeze from either
side, FLQ or Ottawa, could easily upset the diplomatic balance

precariously established by the prime minister through this declaration.

It is doubtful, of course, to what degree the public situation established by the statement reflected the private one. Federal ministers have insisted that there could never have been any consideration of a trade of prisoners,[16] and that may indeed have been Ottawa's position on the evening of October 11. It may also have been Mr. Bourassa's position, and almost certainly was Mr. Choquette's. The federal government may have tolerated Mr. Bourassa's ambiguity simply out of respect for his terrible personal dilemma, and out of a desire to give him and his cabinet a little time to accept the policy of intransigence. Or Ottawa's position, too, may have become momentarily uncertain as a result of the Laporte kidnapping. But if the federal government still was intransigent, the statement created the fresh risk that the public and the FLQ might accept Bourassa's words in good faith, and assume that negotiation leading to an exchange of prisoners and the release of Cross and Laporte was about to begin. The executive council of the Parti Québecois, for example, supported Mr. Bourassa's apparent willingness to negotiate, and warned that the government now had to move quickly to free the hostages.[17] It did not need to stretch the prime minister's words to take this interpretation from them. If Bourassa himself had been speaking in good faith, he might henceforth find himself negotiating ahead of what Ottawa was initially prepared to accept. He would then face the prospect either of convincing Ottawa to move with him, or of betraying his own agreement to negotiate. If, somehow, his government had carried discussion with the FLQ to the point of a deal that the "political prisoners" should be sent into exile, and if this bargain had been publicly declared, Premier Bourassa might have found himself in a position where a veto by Ottawa would have been highly dangerous for Ottawa as for Quebec. With strong enough determination on his part, and the support of his cabinet and any considerable element of the Quebec public, he could have faced Prime Minister Trudeau with an offer to exchange prisoners from a position of real political advantage. By taking the public initiative he did on October 11, Robert Bourassa began to move in that direction. But if he failed to carry through, or if he showed himself to be insincere, the consequences for Quebec would be shattering. One week late, the prime minister of Quebec tentatively assumed public leadership in the crisis; but now the stakes were very high. Would Robert Bourassa be permitted by Ottawa, and would he have the steadiness himself, to establish the terms of a settlement with the FLQ which would release Cross and Laporte?

The response to Mr. Bourassa from the FLQ was immediate. Three communications, from the Chenier cell holding Mr. Laporte, from Laporte himself, and from Mr. Cross were in the hands of the authorities by Monday morning, October 12. An additional communiqué from the Chenier cell was received on Monday afternoon.[18] The opening paragraph of the first message from the cell noted that it was replying "following the tacit acceptance of the demands of the Front by the government of Quebec." The communiqué declared that all negotiation on the substance of the original demands was refused; that the FLQ designated the lawyer Robert Lemieux as its intermediary in discussion of "the technical means of applying the six conditions"; that no new deadline was being suggested, but that "if you show lack of good faith obviously we will act"; and "any hesitation by you will be considered as a tacit refusal and will lead to the execution of Pierre Laporte."[19]

On the crucial matter of "mechanisms" of guarantee, this note said:

> The only guarantee that we can give as far as the freeing of Pierre Laporte is concerned, is our word as Quebec revolutionaries. He will be released safe and sound in the twenty-four hours following fulfillment of the FLQ demands.[20]

The two letters from the kidnap victims emphasized the same point. Mr. Cross wrote:

> As for the guarantees you request concerning my release in good health by the FLQ "Liberation Cell" I can only say that personally I have complete confidence that they will

keep their promise to release me in the twenty-four hours following the successful return to Quebec of the observers accompanying the consenting political prisoners and their wives and families.

You must understand that the FLQ cannot be more specific as to the modalities of my release without compromising their own security.[21]

Mr. Laporte said:

You were asking, with reason, guarantees about the freedom of Mr. Cross and myself. You were right. I am ready unconditionally to accept the word of my kidnappers and I ask of you to do as much.[22]

This three-pronged reply constituted the FLQ's precise and unmistakable answer to Premier Bourassa's proposal to discuss means of guaranteeing the safety of the two hostages as a prerequisite and counterpart to the release of prisoners. By the nature of the situation, all that the FLQ could offer was its word that it would act in good faith if the governments released the prisoners. It might have said so in private discussion, but the offer could not have held any more certainty if it had been made in private. There was more likelihood that a public declaration before the entire country would be sustained than a private one, because the FLQ had its reputation for revolutionary morality to create and sustain. Before any private talks began, the Bourassa and Trudeau governments were thus faced with the basic problem of whether to accept the word of the FLQ and proceed on that assumption, or whether to reject it. If they rejected it, there was no basis for any negotiation. All that the FLQ could do to persuade them of its sincerity would be to repeat the promise. The terrorists' interpretation of any talks that might follow was that they would be solely concerned with the technical means of arranging the freeing of prisoners and the satisfaction of the other demands. There could be no further discussion of guarantees, or of any hypothetical counteroffers that might be made by the governments.

The position of the FLQ on the two kidnappings was slightly

refined in the second note from the Chenier cell received on the afternoon of October 12. It declared that Mr. Cross would be released on the liberation of the "political prisoners" and the suspension of police searches; but that Mr. Laporte would be held until satisfaction of the six remaining original conditions. The note analysed the possibilities arising out of this refinement:

1. The government refuses all the demands, or hesitates to meet them, or takes too much time to answer. Faced with such a situation the two hostages will be executed.

2. The government decides to accept two conditions: liberation of the political prisoners, an end to police operations. In this case, James Cross will be freed during the twenty-four hours following the return of the three observers and the execution of Pierre Laporte will be lifted, unless the police forces find the whereabouts of Pierre Laporte. But the minister of unemployment and assimilation of Quebeckers will not be freed.

3. The government decides to meet the six original demands of the FLQ. In this case Pierre Laporte and James Cross will be let go safe and sound within the twenty-four hours following the complete realization of the liberation operation.

This communiqué is the last from the Chenier cell before the execution or liberation of Pierre Laporte. The scope of the situation is clear. All obstinacy, all delay will be considered a tacit refusal.[23]

If the governments had been prepared to accept negotiation in good faith, leading to the release of prisoners, the strong possibility existed at this stage that Mr. Cross would regain his liberty and Mr. Laporte would be held indefinitely but not killed. If they were not prepared to bargain in good faith, there was no reason whatever (except the slight hope that the police might still quickly rescue the hostages without injury) to believe that the lives of Cross and Laporte could be saved. The entry into bargaining could only confirm the impression of the governments' good faith, and once created, that impression would

have a powerful influence on the political atmosphere. A retreat from negotiation would henceforward be justifiably regarded as a betrayal of two men's lives—unless it followed
clear public evidence of the FLQ's bad faith, or unless the
retreat were somehow camouflaged under a larger diversion.

Premier Bourassa, by naming Robert Demers as negotiator
to speak for the government in talks with Mr. Lemieux, took
the next ominous step. He maintained the appearance of good
faith by instructing his delegate to deal with the FLQ.[24] The
price of deceit in negotiation was mounting steadily.

And the situation was growing complex. Under the stress of
more than a week of crisis, a series of official concessions, a
second kidnapping, and the continuing absence of any formal
public reassurance by the country's leaders, public opinion was
increasingly splintered and confused.[25] In Montreal, there was
evidence of considerable support for a negotiated exchange of
"political prisoners" for the two hostages. A public opinion
poll on the crisis taken in the city on October 15 and 16, in
which an unusual proportion of thirty-nine percent of those
approached refused to be interviewed (the polling organization
reported that the normal "refusal rate" was about ten percent),
revealed that forty-six percent of the respondents favoured
transporting the twenty-three prisoners to Cuba or Algeria to
save the lives of Cross and Laporte.[26] *Le Devoir* reasserted its
editorial opinion that the hostages' lives should be saved by an
exchange.[27]

Other organizations in the province, moving to fill the vacu-
um in political leadership, were making much more ambiguous
declarations about the FLQ manifesto. The Front d'action politique (FRAP), the coalition of citizens' committees and labour groups contesting the Montreal civic election in opposition to the Drapeau Civic Party slate, declared its support for
the "objectives" of the FLQ in a rally on Sunday evening,
October 11.[28] Two days later, the Montreal executive committee of the Confederation of National Trade Unions, under the
chairmanship of the nationalist Michel Chartrand, issued a
similar statement of support.[29] Mr. Chartrand added that the
provincial government was seeking "to start a fateful panic

among the Quebec people" which could lead to a breakdown
of discussion with the FLQ and the imposition of a "police
state" upon the province. In his provocative press conference,
Chartrand affirmed the CNTU's conviction that the FLQ
threatened only "the dominating minority which is at the
source of the ills from which Quebec is currently suffering." He
volunteered that the Montreal CNTU would provide body-
guards for the two leading propagandists of the FLQ, Pierre
Vallières and Charles Gagnon.[30] The same day, student leaders in the city's CEGEPs (or community colleges) announced
their intention of calling student strikes in support of the aims
of the FLQ on Wednesday, October 14. To politicians who
opposed any effective concession to the terrorists, but who
were still temporizing, these contagious events could only sig-
nify a worrying disintegration of their political authority.
From this perspective, it was natural that more and more desperate consideration would be given to the problem of how to
reassert political authority.

But there was another approach to the problem of the FLQ's
challenge to constitutional authority which was canvassed urgently during these days. In retrospect, it was maligned vaguely
as being subversive and revolutionary by Jean Drapeau, and
condemned by anonymous members of the federal Liberal administration. Prime Minister Trudeau regarded it at the least as
naive; and it finally became one factor (of indeterminate
weight) in the evidence considered by the Drapeau, Bourassa
and Trudeau governments which led them to agree to the imposition of War Measures.[31] But in conception it was entirely
legitimate and constructive (although its acceptance would
have resulted in a profound change in the balance and direction
of the Quebec provincial government). This was the approach
represented by Claude Ryan, the editor of *Le Devoir*. It began
from the assumption that saving the lives of the hostages was
the first consideration, from the judgment that this could only
be assured by negotiations to free the "political prisoners," and
from a concern that the crisis should be resolved by the Quebec
government rather than by Ottawa. Given these goals, Ryan
and the editorial board of *Le Devoir* examined in private how

they could be achieved while maintaining political order and
the authority of the state.

In a later editorial, Ryan recalled the discussion held by his
editorial board on Sunday, October 11, after Mr. Laporte's
kidnapping. The group considered what developments might
occur in the situation, and reduced them to three: first, that the
Bourassa government, "under pressure from Ottawa and Montreal, would give in to the temptation of having the War Measures Act invoked immediately, thus passing the primary responsibility for the crisis to Ottawa even though the Quebec
government was the most directly involved." The editors did
not favour this outcome. Second, they considered whether, under the pressure of further terrorism, the Bourassa government
might be "reduced to impotence and reveal itself incapable of
controlling the situation." In that event, they concluded that
the government would have to strengthen itself "out of the
most valuable elements of the various provincial parties, reinforced by some political personalities from different milieu."
And finally, they considered

> the possibility that the Bourassa government, deciding to
> find a solution through negotiations, and thus opting for
> the complete affirmation of its responsibilities, would
> emerge from the crisis more unified and self-confident. In
> this event, however, we felt that at the end of the crisis Mr.
> Bourassa would still have to reinforce his cabinet team.[32]

The editorial board of *Le Devoir* considered this third possibility as "the most plausible and realistic." Following discussion
of the three hypotheses with Lucien Saulnier and others by
telephone, Mr. Ryan and his colleagues awaited "the unfolding
of events."[33]

> The next morning I again spoke with my colleagues. We
> took note of Mr. Bourassa's speech broadcast the previous
> evening, and of Mr. Saulnier's opinion. Mr. Bourassa with
> his speech had opened up a new avenue for negotiations
> and so we decided without any discussion to drop the two
> other possibilities and to support the stand taken by the

leader of the Government. This option seemed to us all the
more imperative as we knew, from a good source, that the
members of his cabinet were divided on the question, that
Jerome Choquette was threatening to resign and that the
stand taken by Mr. Bourassa on October 11 seemed the
most humane and realistic. On Oct. 13 I wrote an editorial
supporting this stand.[34]

Claude Ryan's position was intended as one of *support* for a
Quebec government committed to negotiation, and *reinforcement* of that government from other parties in order that it
might carry through its tentatively declared policy without
being politically undermined, either by opponents within the
cabinet such as Mr. Choquette, by opponents in the Montreal
civic administration or in Ottawa, or by an FLQ that would be
certain to boast of its victory. The instinct to seek reinforcement of a government in the face of severe challenge is a natural one for parliamentary democrats, arising out of a belief that
the defence of partisan distinctions is less fundamental than the
defence of the state's authority.[35] The accusation, or the hint,
that a proposal for coalition in crisis is subversive can only
arise out of panic, or malice, or dogmatic commitment to a
partisan position which could not be upheld by such a coalition.
   In assessing the forces at work after the Laporte kidnapping,
it is vital to understand that Claude Ryan's very tentative initiative was taken in defence of constituted authority, not in defiance of it. His editorial of October 13 favouring negotiations
arose directly out of Mr. Bourassa's indication the previous
evening that he wished to enter negotiations. His private
suggestion of a broadened cabinet was intended to give the
government the self-confidence to sustain these negotiations to
the point of success.
   While Mr. Ryan did not discuss the possibility of a broadened government with René Lévesque, the leader of the Parti
Québecois, it was evident at the time that the leaders of that
party were prepared to stand behind Prime Minister Bourassa
in the policy of negotiation. Mr. Lévesque indicated this pri-

vately to the premier when they met before Mr. Bourassa's radio address on Sunday evening, October 11; he reasserted the commitment publicly the same evening; and other members of the party renewed the commitment in meetings with Mr. Bourassa during the week.[16] For an independentist party fundamentally opposed to the federalist stance of the Quebec government, this was a significant and generous commitment; from a party commanding twenty-four percent of the popular vote the previous April, it was an offer of cooperation that should not have been taken lightly. The commitment of support applied whether or not the Bourassa government would take the PQ into coalition; its sole condition was that the Quebec government should negotiate a settlement of the crisis without inviting the intervention of Ottawa. This seemed to the Parti Québécois to be the course of greatest prudence for Quebec, the policy least likely to create political chaos and prolonged disturbance in the province.[37]

While the constellation favouring negotiation was forming behind what was judged to be the Quebec government's position, other events pointed to a different dénouement. There was discussion among federal Liberal MPs and ministers of the use of emergency powers against the FLQ; the possibility certainly arose in discussions on October 11 among Mr. Trudeau, Mr. Bourassa, Mr. Drapeau and Mr. Saulnier.[38] The federal government was giving signs of impatience and a new willingness to use a big stick; and that, when it was applied, would mean the end of negotiation between Quebec and the FLQ. On October 12, the minister of defence, Donald Macdonald, confirmed the arrival in Ottawa, at the request of the R.C.M.P, of units of the Canadian Armed Forces. Their assignment, he noted, was to guard federal buildings and public figures (on the Ontario side of the Ottawa River).[39] There were unofficial reports in the next two days of troop movements to bases near Montreal.[40]

Both these events could be explained as routine provision for assistance to the police forces, which were understandably reporting strain after several days of unrelieved and unrewarded activity. But Prime Minister Trudeau's off-the-cuff remarks in a long exchange with the CBC television reporter Tim

Ralfe on October 13 suggested other intentions. The prime minister vigorously defended the attempt to forestall further kidnappings by use of the army; and toward the end of the interview, under persistent questioning, he moved well beyond this issue to some general considerations.

> You know, I think it is . . . important to get rid of those who are committing violence against the total society and those who are trying to run the government through a parallel power by establishing their authority by kidnapping and blackmail. And I think it is our duty as a government to protect government officials and important people in our society against being used as tools in this blackmail. Now, you don't agree to this but I am sure that, once again with hindsight, you would probably have found it preferable if Mr. Cross and Mr. Laporte had been protected from kidnapping, which they weren't because these steps we're taking now weren't taken. But even with your hindsight I don't see how you can deny that.

Question: No, I still go back to the choice that you have to make in the kind of society that you live in.

Trudeau: Yes, well there are a lot of bleeding hearts around who just don't like to see people with helmets and guns. All I can say is, go on and bleed, but it is more important to keep law and order in the society than to be worried about weak-kneed people who don't like the looks of . . .

Question: At any cost? How far would you go with that? How far would you extend that?

Trudeau: Well, just watch me.

Question: At reducing civil liberties? To what extent?

Trudeau: To what extent?

Question: Well, if you extend this and you say, OK, you're going to do anything to protect them, does this include wiretapping, reducing other civil liberties in some way?

Trudeau: Yes, I think the society must take every means at its disposal to defend itself against the emergence of a parallel power which defies the elected power in this country and I think that goes to any distance. So long as there is a power in here which is challenging the elected representatives of the people, I think that power must be stopped and I think it's only, I repeat, weak-kneed bleeding hearts who are afraid to take these measures.[41]

These comments did not leave the impression that the prime minister was interested in serious negotiation with the FLQ.

Meanwhile the two negotiators, Lemieux and Demers, met on Tuesday and Wednesday, October 13 and 14 to discuss terms, but could not advance beyond preliminaries. The Quebec government apparently requested two hostages from the kidnapping cells to be held until the release of Cross and Laporte.[42] The two cells replied in a public communiqué the next day that they could not accept the request; instead, the FLQ could "only renew its solemn commitment before the people of Quebec."[43]

On Wednesday, the point of crisis approached rapidly. Premier Bourassa indicated to Claude Ryan (and perhaps to René Lévesque) that "there would be a 'slight turn' toward firmness."[44] In Toronto, Prime Minister John Robarts of Ontario spoke for the opponents of compromise when he declared that:

There is no way we can yield to these terrorist demands. . . By Jove, this has got to be a law-abiding country where you can bring your family up without fear . . . the demands are wrong—morally wrong and socially wrong—we have to stand and fight. It's war—total war.[45]

These two indications of hardening attitudes led Ryan, Lévesque, the executive of the Parti Québecois and a number of Quebec labour leaders and scholars to denounce Premier Robarts' intervention, and jointly to urge Premier Bourassa to free the convicts in return for the safety of Cross and Laporte.[46] At this point of growing confusion, the joint statement may have helped finally to turn the governments away from bargaining. The declaration could easily be linked, in the increasingly paranoiac atmosphere, with the earlier distorted accounts which had reached Ottawa and Quebec City of Ryan's discussion of a broadened Quebec government. Public tensions were now so high, and the boldness of the FLQ's spokesmen and supporters on radio and television and in the colleges and universities of Quebec was now so potentially explosive, that the continuation of negotiation much longer might perhaps have helped to precipitate demonstrations and some disorder in Montreal.[47]

To Jean Drapeau and Lucien Saulnier, from their narrow perspective in Montreal City Hall, that possibility must have seemed a certainty. It may have been too late for any action on the part of the governments other than a dramatic renunciation of compromise; but even at this late hour, if the will to negotiate had existed, a quick settlement might still have broken the immediate tension.

But the will was not there. Sometime in the two or three days before October 16, Prime Minister Trudeau, Premier Bourassa and Mayor Drapeau had agreed that the pretence of dealing with the FLQ would be ended, the lives of Cross and Laporte would be finally risked, and War Measures would be imposed to give the police the special powers of search and arrest they had been seeking and to shock the Quebec public out of its confusion into support for established authority. After a patently disingenuous offer to the FLQ on Thursday evening, October 15, at 9 P.M. (to recommend parole for five terrorist prisoners who were due for parole), with a demand for a reply by 3 A.M. the following morning, the three leaders agreed upon the immediate imposition of War Measures. At 4 A.M. on Friday, October 16, 1970, the Public Order Regulations (1970), issued under the War Measures Act, went into force in Canada. From that moment, the lives of the two hostages were abandoned in the interest of larger reasons of state.

The difficulties of coordination and political reconciliation among three levels of government were patently demonstrated during the crisis. Three governments, each with its own electorate, its own traditions, it own balance of personalities, its own normal range of authority, were suddenly thrust together and forced to work out a common policy aimed at meeting all their disparate purposes in the crisis. The uncertainties and delays which were the features of policy from October 5 to October 16 were partly the result of this interplay. Jurisdictions were not clearly divided, and could not easily be sorted out; constant consultations among the three leaders were necessary (as among their civil and police subordinates), and when there was uncertainty or disagreement from one source, and a reluctance or inability to force a decision on the part of the others, the result could only be—delay. Delay itself thus became policy, and allowed the growth of public suspense, distraction, division, and confusion. In the end, in the judgment of all three governments, that public condition became the most dangerous element in the whole affair, and the one unifying threat which permitted (or dictated) the emergence of a common policy. But the common policy permitted by the situation was blunt and undiscriminating. In the short run it might bring order through shock; in the long run it was likely to intensify the disease.

Was delay the inevitable outcome of the federal division of responsibilities? Or could one government at any point have taken a different lead than it did and expect to carry the others with it?

There is no doubt that the Drapeau-Saulnier administration in Montreal opposed dealing with the terrorists on any terms at any time. But Montreal had no formal constitutional role in policy-making; and they kept out of any public involvement during the first week after the Cross kidnapping. In that initial period, the other two governments might have been able to act while disregarding the views of Drapeau and Saulnier. (Though they would have been castigated privately for doing so if they had compromised with the terrorists.) If the decision had been to reject the demands of the terrorists completely (and without alternative offers), Ottawa and Quebec City would have had the full support of the Montreal government. Why, then, did Ottawa not do so?

The explanation may be a simple one: while it is easy to express a hard instinctive response to terror, it is not so easy to act upon that instinct when a life is at stake. The hardness remained; it was softened by humanity. For several days the Trudeau government lacked the complete ruthlessness of its instincts. To reject the demands of the terrorists bluntly and quickly would have required a willful hardening of the heart, and a readiness to reveal this hardening to the Canadian public. Rather than admitting to such a cruel will, fairness suggests that the members of the government preferred to seek time: because time might bring other solutions, and because it would allow some preparation for the dismay a hard decision might create. An uncompromising choice rested, in the first week, with the Trudeau government alone: that it hesitated is some credit to its moral sense. When Pierre Trudeau, the self-disciplinarian, finally burst out against the bleeding hearts on October 13 it may have been his own sense of humanity he was exorcising.

But the hesitations of the second week seemed more complicated. By this time, Ottawa appeared hardened to a tragic outcome. The federal government could not, however, simply impose its will on a Quebec government whose senior minister was under sentence of death. Considerations of political prudence as well as decency required deference to Robert Bourassa in the aftermath of Pierre Laporte's kidnapping. So, a distraught Premier was given the lead for a few days, to show whether he could somehow avert the terrible conclusion threatened by the FLQ—but apparently without the freedom to negotiate realistically on the crucial issue. Once again, it is difficult to draw conclusions about motives; but the same conflict of conscience—even more intense—may have torn Bourassa and his associates in the second week as apparently affected the Trudeau government in the first. The federal structure meant that the country had to bear two consecutive trials of conscience and will by different governments in the same crisis; and added together, the two periods of suspense and uncertainty brought an ominous degeneration of public morale and sense of direction.

The awkwardnesses of the federal system were thus a factor in the deteriorating situation; but this is not to say that a unitary system would necessarily have done much to prevent the degeneration that occurred. Indecisiveness in the highly centralized Fifth French Republic brought France to the same state of confusion in the days of May, 1968. And decisiveness in Ottawa alone in the first week, either in favour of a trade of prisoners or against it, would have cut the tension. The difficulties of the federal relationship came to the fore most dangerously after the imposition of War Measures rather than before.

3: The vicious game

When it invoked the War Measures Act for the first time in peacetime, the federal government made two concessions to political prudence which were legally unnecessary. The Act is a federal statute, brought into force by order-in-council; its proclamation requires the approval neither of the provinces nor of Parliament. But in its care to minimize criticism and demonstrate its cooperation with the Quebec authorities, Ottawa arranged for letters requesting extraordinary measures to be sent from Quebec City and Montreal City Hall before the proclamation of emergency powers. These were received in Ottawa after midnight on October 15-16. And on Friday morning, October 16, the government introduced a resolution in the House of Commons seeking the House's approval of its action.[1] The resolution stated that approval was to be granted "on the clear understanding" that the proclamation would be revoked on or before April 30, 1971, unless the House adopted a further resolution extending emergency powers beyond that date.

The letters of request from Premier Bourassa, Mayor Drapeau and Chairman Saulnier demonstrated the common front of Ottawa, Quebec City and Montreal, and indicated a shared moral responsibility for the use of emergency powers. The resolution presented to the House of Commons sought immediate reinforcement for the cabinet's decision from the House, before any members of the opposition could take the opportunity to introduce a resolution of censure.[2] Both Quebec and the House were sensitive about their roles in the crisis; these two steps were politically shrewd means for the federal cabinet to fend off accusations of unilateral and arbitrary action on its part. Henceforth, members of the government frequently asserted, as justification for the use of War Measures, that Ottawa had acted reluctantly and upon request, and that the cabinet had the overwhelming support of the House of Commons in its action. But in spite of such political precautions (which the government made good use of), final responsibility for War Measures rested with Prime Minister Trudeau and his cabinet; and that responsibility requires assessment. The requests from Quebec, and the House's *ex post facto* approval, are only secondary justifications for the extraordinary suspension of liberties that occurred. The substantive case presented by the Trudeau government is what must be judged against the evidence.

Section two of the War Measures Act provides that:

> The issue of a proclamation by Her Majesty, or under the authority of the Governor in Council shall be conclusive evidence that war, invasion, or insurrection, real or apprehended, exists and has existed for any period of time therein stated, and of its continuance, until by the issue of a further proclamation it is declared that the war, invasion or insurrection no longer exists.[3]

Section three of the Act grants unrestricted authority (superceding the normal, federal distribution of legislative powers under the B.N.A. Act, the guarantees of civil liberties under the Canadian Bill of Rights, and the general legislative authority of the federal Parliament) to the federal cabinet to make the orders and regulations it deems necessary to deal with the emergency it has defined in the proclamation. The remaining sections provide for penalties and elaborate upon certain procedures under the Act.[4]

The letter from Prime Minister Bourassa requesting emergency measures referred to "a concerted effort to intimidate and overthrow the government and the democratic institutions of this province through planned and systematic illegal action, including insurrection."[5] Lucien Saulnier and Jean Drapeau, in their joint letter, spoke of the need to protect society "against the seditious plot and the apprehended insurrection in which the kidnappings were the first step."[6] The federal proclamation of War Measures, the press release announcing it, and the government's resolution before the House all referred to "the state of apprehended insurrection."[7] Since the Act restricts action under its provisions in the case of an internal crisis to a period of "insurrection, real or apprehended," the governments had to base their defence of its use upon the claim that insurrection existed. Legally, the Act provides that the proclamation itself shall be sufficient evidence of the existence of a crisis: that is, the courts are explicitly prevented from hearing any challenge to the proclamation.[8] But politically, the necessity remained for the governments to offer some defence of their acts.

The public overwhelmingly and uncritically accepted this defence. Did that acceptance reflect the soundness of the governments' case? Or did it, rather, reflect extreme public anxiety (and in some cases panic), a Canadian disposition to defer to authority, and a tenuous tradition of dissent? There are other, related questions. Is the evidence sufficient to make a judgment about whether or not an "apprehended insurrection" really existed? If no insurrection existed, was it nevertheless legitimate for the governments to claim that one did in order technically to justify the invocation of War Measures? Did the governments require special powers to meet the challenge of the FLQ? Could these powers have been acquired by more limited and more palatable means? Was the use of emergency powers politically wise?

The special powers actually taken up by the federal cabinet under War Measures were defined in the Public Order Regulations, 1970.[9] These regulations declared the Front de Libération du Québec, any successor group or association, "or any group of persons or association that advocates the use of force or the commission of crime as a means of or as an aid in accomplishing governmental change within Canada," to be an unlawful association. Holding office or membership in, com-

munication on behalf of, advocacy of the aims or principles of,
financial contributions to, assistance to, and the provision of
housing for, members of the outlawed associations were declared offences under the Regulations, subject to penalties of
up to five years in prison. (In the case of providing housing for
members or promoters of the outlawed associations, there was
an additional liability to a maximum fine of $5,000.) Under the
Regulations, and in the absence of evidence to the contrary,
attendance at any meeting of the outlawed associations, public
advocacy of the associations, or the communication of statements on their behalf, was to be taken as proof of membership.
The Regulations gave power to law officers to arrest suspected
persons and to search premises without warrant, to seize property, to deny bail (unless specific consent to bail was granted by
the provincial attorney general), to hold persons without
charge for a maximum of twenty-one days, and to hold without
trial for a maximum of ninety days.

   The Regulations thus created a new and retroactive criminal
offence of membership in an unlawful association, and established a range of unusual police powers of search, arrest and
detention. Later, in December, the application of the War
Measures Act and Regulations was lifted on passage through
the regular legislative process of the Public Order (Temporary
Measures) Act, 1970; this Act retained (with some refinements)
the essential features of the original Regulations, but it did not
depend for its defence upon the claimed existence of apprehended insurrection. It is evident that, in some senses, the
question of the existence of a state of insurrection on October
16 is a separate one from the question of whether any new
criminal offences or special police powers were necessary for
the authorities to meet the threat posed by the FLQ.

   Prime Minister Trudeau made two defences of War Measures on October 16, the first in the House of Commons and
the second on national television that evening. He was supported in the House in major statements by the minister of justice,
Mr. Turner; the minister of regional economic expansion, Mr.
Marchand; and the minister of labour, Mr. Mackasey.[10] These
statements, the letters from Quebec City and Montreal tabled

by the prime minister, and certain *obiter dicta* about the crisis by Prime Minister Bourassa and Mayor Drapeau constitute the core of the arguments offered to the Canadian public in defence of the proclamation of War Measures. During the following week, Mr. Trudeau was repeatedly pressed in the House of Commons to reveal what confidential information the government had considered in reaching its decision. On October 23 the leader of the New Democratic Party, T. C. Douglas, asked Mr. Trudeau whether he would give this information to the House, or privately give it to the opposition party leaders, or indicate to the House whether he desired to postpone any statement on the matter. The prime minister made an emphatic reply:

> By now I would have thought this information was in the hands of everybody. We have at various times explained why the War Measures Act was brought in at the time it was. The first fact was that there had been kidnappings of two very important people in Canada and that they were being held for ransom under the threat of death. The second was that the government of the province of Quebec and the authorities of the city of Montreal asked the federal government to permit the use of exceptional measures because, in their own words, a state of apprehended insurrection existed. The third reason was our assessment of all the surrounding facts, which are known to the country by now—the state of confusion that existed in the province of Quebec in regard to these matters.[11]

Mr. Douglas then asked whether there was any evidence "of a conspiracy to bring about an insurrection," and of the claim made by Jean Marchand "that there were thousands of rifles, machine guns and bombs in the possession of the FLQ." Did the government have such information, or was it simply acting upon "statements made to it by other authorities?" The prime minister elaborated:

> I repeat, Mr. Speaker, not entirely on the recommendations made by other authorities, though that was obviously

an important element in our decision. When the authorities of the province of Quebec and the city of Montreal say that there is a state of apprehended insurrection existing, then we take that statement to be a serious one. They are elected by the people and are responsible governments. But that is not the only source of information; of course it is not. There are other facts which have been made known to the public—that a great quantity of dynamite has been stolen in Quebec during the last year and not recovered, that there is a great quantity—I do not know the exact number but at any rate it is substantial—of rifles and small arms that have disappeared.

I wish the leader of the New Democratic Party would ask himself how much information Kerensky had in the spring and summer of 1917 when he was pooh-poohing the possibility of an insurrection which in fact happened in October, 1917.[12]

Mr. Stanfield, the Progressive Conservative leader, took the next step, seeking renewed confirmation that "the public had available to it the information upon which the government based its decision." Mr. Trudeau replied:

Mr. Speaker, what I said was that the facts that I have recited and which are known to the House were sufficient for us to take the steps we did. I am not saying that beyond that there are not other facts which may or may not be known to the public. It is a matter that will be left to the police, as far as I am concerned. I say that the facts that are known to the House are the facts on which we acted, and it is on that that we stand.[13]

There was, apparently, no more certain evidence of "insurrection" than had already been revealed by late October.[14]

In his statement to the House of Commons on October 16, the prime minister tabled the official letters requesting emergency measures, reviewed briefly the background to the government's decision, and reported upon the police raids and arrests that had occurred since the proclamations at 4 A.M. that

morning. The letter from Prime Minister Bourassa noted the
great shock to the Quebec public occasioned by the kidnappings,

> as well as by the threats to the security of the state and
> individuals expressed in communiqués issued by the
> Front de Libération du Québec or on its behalf, and final-
> ly all the circumstances surrounding these events.[15]

The Quebec government was concerned, said Mr. Bourassa, to
"be able to put an immediate stop to intimidation and terror
and to ensure peace and security for all citizens." To do so, it
was convinced that special police powers of arrest and detention were necessary,

> to apprehend and keep in custody individuals who, the
> attorney general of Quebec has valid reasons to believe,
> are determined to overthrow the government through vio-
> lence and illegal means.[16]

The letter from the Montreal leaders made the same point
about the general threat of insurrection. It was accompanied by
a letter from the director of the Montreal Police Department,
M. St.-Pierre, which emphasized that broader powers were
needed—not to continue the search for the two hostages—but
rather to suppress an incipient uprising:

> The recent kidnappings of a foreign diplomat and of a
> minister of the Crown of the province of Quebec by this
> organization are the first stage of its seditious plan and of
> activities leading directly to insurrection and the over-
> throw of the State.
>
> Under the circumstances the investigation which
> must be carried out by police authorities must necessarily
> include all the activities of the various cells of this sedi-
> tious organization and should not be restricted, if it is not
> to be doomed to failure to a mere search for the individu-
> als who have perpetrated the heinous kidnapping of the
> two persons who are still being held.
>
> The threat to our society from this seditious conspira-

cy that has swung into action in the last eleven days, the investigation problems created by the internal structure of this organization divided into many small autonomous cells and the incredible amount of checking and searching imposed upon us have taxed and are taxing to the utmost the resources available to our police department.

The extreme urgency of obtaining concrete results in uncovering all the ramifications of this organization and its seditious activities, the volume and complexity of the evidence to be gathered and filed, finally the enormous task that we must carry out without resorting to unhealthy and undesirable repression, make it essential for higher levels of government to come to our assistance if we are to succeed.[17]

What was begun on October 16, in the eyes of the Quebec authorities, was no "mere search" for the kidnappers. As much as the governments might say they regretted it, the two hostages were now seen as relatively insignificant pawns in a much broader struggle to maintain the integrity of the state. This was the case accepted by Prime Minister Trudeau. His own justification for War Measures was short and straightforward:

In recent years we have been forced to acknowledge the existence within Canada of a new and terrifying type of person—one who in earlier times would have been described as an anarchist, but who is now known as a violent revolutionary. These persons allege that they are seeking social change through novel means. In fact they are seeking the destruction of the social order through clandestine and violent means.

Faced with such persons, and confronted with authoritative assessments of the seriousness of the risk to persons and property in the Montreal area, the government had no responsible choice but to act as it did last night. Given the rapid deterioration of the situation as mentioned by Prime Minister Bourassa, and given the expiration of the time offered for the release of the hostages, it became obvious

that the urgency of the situation demanded rapid action.
The absence both of adequate time to take other steps or
of alternative legislative authority dictated the use of the
War Measures Act.[18]

A variety of phrases had been used to describe the "apprehended insurrection." The director of the Montreal Police had
spoken of "activities leading directly to insurrection;" Mr.
Bourassa mentioned a "concerted effort" to overthrow the government by force; Mr. Drapeau and Mr. Saulnier referred to
"the apprehended insurrection in which the recent kidnappings
were the first step." More vaguely, Prime Minister Bourassa
spoke of the condition of public anxiety and of "all the circumstances surrounding these events," and Prime Minister Trudeau
noted "the rapid deterioration of the situation." No one in
authority, to this point, had offered fresh evidence of a plan or
conspiracy to overthrow the Quebec government. There were
"first steps," there was anticipation, there was a "deteriorating
situation;" but what decisive evidence, beyond the circumstances of two kidnappings and a series of bold FLQ communiqués, led the governments to foresee civil insurrection? How
did they make the leap from kidnapping to revolution?

Following Prime Minister Trudeau's brief statement, the
Hon. John N. Turner made the comprehensive case for the
government's action. He began by admitting that the problem
for governments of "balancing the rights of individual citizens
against the rights of society as a whole" always involved "a
question of judgment in each individual case." There was room
for discretion, Mr. Turner admitted; and this implied that the
government might conceivably be mistaken. This admission of
fallibility suggests that the cabinet did not possess any definitive evidence of imminent insurrection, but rather that it used
its judgment in a quite speculative way, taking into account the
public events of the previous ten days.

Mr. Turner's next statements add strength to this interpretation of the cabinet's approach. He fell back upon the prime
minister's initial, unyielding response to blackmail.

Surrender would simply have inflated the ego and whetted

the appetite of the FLQ, while at the same time enervating and eroding the will of governments and society to resist the encroachments of these criminals.[19]

Any exchange of prisoners "would merely have invited escalation. . . . And there would have been no stop to it." Ottawa was clearly nervous, that is, about the maintenance of the state's authority, and its conception of authority would not permit serious negotiation with the kidnappers. If the pretended process of bargaining with the FLQ had been entered into in doubt and uncertainty, the experience of it had confirmed that it should not be carried to a conclusion. (That was not a surprising conclusion for Ottawa to come to. The failure of false diplomacy is predetermined, but it may serve to reassure closed minds that they were right.) Said Mr. Turner:

> There had been a recent and rapid escalation. I believe that the climate that had been set by an attempt to negotiate, by the vocabulary which had been adopted of "political prisoners," the use of the word "execution" of those who had been kidnapped instead of "murder," as if to imply some legitimacy, placed the government in a position of immobility whereby all the action in terms of public opinion was left to a bunch of renegades and the government was having difficulty sustaining its position.[20]

The argument here took a crucial shift. Mr. Turner was not asserting the existence of a general FLQ plot or conspiracy, but the degeneration of public confidence in and respect for established authority. The Minister re-emphasized the importance of this consideration, noting once again the "rapid acceleration" of a dangerous situation. The kidnappings and the inflammatory messages of the FLQ, added to the record of previous bombings and thefts of dynamite, had led to something "more disturbing . . . a type of erosion of the public will in the feeling among some sincere people that an exchange of prisoners for the victims of the kidnappings would somehow ease the situation." This "erosion of will" was linked by Mr. Turner to the provocations of those sympathetic to the FLQ:

> I might say, too, that the recent call for a public manifesta-
> tion by men like Gagnon, Vallières and Chartrand estab-
> lished and escalated the whole coming together of an infil-
> tration of FLQ doctrine in certain areas of society in
> Quebec—in the unions, among universities and in the me-
> dia—and the growing feeling among the people of
> Quebec, particularly the citizens of Montreal, that they
> are living under a reign of terror.[21]

Twice in his speech Mr. Turner spoke of the impossibility of
revealing "the full details of the intelligence upon which the
government acted," but in context these were minor asides;
his emphasis was unmistakably on what he saw as the dangerous collapse of public will in Quebec. There might certainly be
additional pieces of information to fit into this pattern, but
the pattern was intelligible as Mr. Turner offered it. Three
weeks later, in introducing the legislation to replace War Measures to the House of Commons, Mr. Turner returned insis-
tently to his original case.

> We do not have to explore plots or allegations of provi-
> sional governments to appreciate the acute sense of ap-
> prehension and fear in Quebec in those days preceding
> the proclamation of the War Measures Act.
>   Those who still continue to suggest that our decision
> had to be based upon some sort of tallying up, some sort
> of mathematical summary of the number of sticks of dyna-
> mite that had been stolen, or the estimate of the number of
> terrorists involved with the FLQ and the number of specif-
> ic instances of violence that had taken place, operate, I
> submit, from a misleading premise. Let there be no mis-
> take: the government recognizes that the decision involved
> a value judgment, it involved an assessment by the govern-
> ment of all the available facts, but the decision of the
> government must be viewed against the total background
> of events in Quebec, events that form a continuum of
> change in the social fabric of that province.[22]

Mr. Turner quoted an American authority in support of his

assertion that the state must not be required to measure danger by any precise scale: "A single revolutionary spark," wrote Justice Edward T. Sanford, "may kindle a fire that, smouldering for a time, may burst into a sweeping and destructive conflagration."[23]

A few other pieces fill out the framework. Robert Bourassa spoke in a CBC television interview of a revolutionary scheme consisting of five phases: demonstrations, bombing, kidnappings, selective assassinations, and urban guerrilla warfare. Three stages of this prophecy seemed to have been fulfilled, and Mr. Bourassa was sufficiently convinced on October 16 that "the plan" was being systematically applied to feel that an exceptional response was necessary.[24] The nature and reliability of Mr. Bourassa's evidence may be in doubt; but there is no doubt that at this stage Mr. Bourassa accepted it as conclusive.[25]

The fragility of his government's reputation among the political élite of Quebec had been brought home to Mr. Bourassa in his telephone conversation with Claude Ryan on Sunday, October 12, when Ryan had urged him to broaden membership in his cabinet from outside his party.[26] The declaration of public figures on Wednesday evening calling for an exchange of prisoners, the apparently burgeoning student demonstrations on Thursday, and the spread of rumour and panic in Montreal, could well be seen by an insecure cabinet in Quebec City as the overture to chaos and collapse. Jean Marchand spoke in febrile language to the House of Commons; and in Montreal after the event, Mayor Drapeau spoke alarmingly of the Ryan proposal as an effort "to set up the provisional government that was to preside over transfer of constitutional authority to a revolutionary regime."[27] Prime Minister Trudeau discussed later the possibility of the crisis leading to fighting in the streets, and a situation like that at Kent State University, in which the police and military might fire on civilians.[28]

Whatever relative weight was given to these factors in invoking War Measures, such nervous speculation was in the air, was mentioned by official sources, and contributed to the mounting sense of crisis. As Mr. Trudeau and Mr. Turner insisted, the government's case is known and needs no further support: there were alarming signals, there was a general assessment of the situation, and on balance the federal government concluded that emergency measures were necessary. They were invoked as a precautionary act, to halt what was seen as a dangerous decay of public authority and to permit the police to go on what has been called a "fishing expedition" against the FLQ and its sympathizers, who might possibly have seized upon a deteriorating situation to create still greater confusion and panic.

Peter C. Newman of the Toronto *Star* summed up the official case in a front page comment on October 30:

> Few revolutions are triggered by a single event—the storming of a barricade, the assassination of a public man, riots in the street. Instead, a series of disjointed incidents converge to create a climate of anarchy, violent ferment that shocks a society into desperate convulsions which eventually overthrow its legitimate authority. Individually, the incidents that took place in Montreal that fateful week might have been contained within the existing legal apparatus. But looking at them together, the Bourassa and Trudeau governments decided, they threatened to destroy Quebec's social order.[29]

The case seems deceptively clear. But it is nevertheless complicated, and its implications are profound. If there is any mystery in why the War Measures Act was proclaimed, the mystery is not contained in some confidential police file on the plans of the Front de Libération du Québec. There was no decisive concealed evidence of an imminent civil uprising. In the ordinary sense of the phrase, there was no "apprehended insurrection."[30] There was rather a pattern of events which was fitted into a preconceived framework or "scenario" by those in authority. The model did not depend for its appropriateness, beyond a certain point, on systematic acts of the FLQ; it involved, instead, the prediction of an infectious series of semi-autonomous actions and responses throughout the body politic leading to a general loss of public respect for established authority, spontaneous or uncontrolled conflict in the streets, division and loss of confidence among those in power, and finally some kind of extraconstitutional coup d'état to install a new political regime.

If anything essential has not yet been revealed in the affair, it is most likely to be further information about the state of near disintegration of the Quebec cabinet in the days before War Measures,[31] and the developing state of mind of all those persons who advised the two prime ministers before October 16. What seems to have happened was that ten days of confusion, federal-provincial consultation, and playing for time put the governments into a psychological condition in which they felt their authority to be slipping away beneath them. In the degenerating climate, there seemed no longer to be any room for manoeuvre or subtlety: either the FLQ would succeed in gaining the release of the "political prisoners" and the authority of the state would collapse; or it would be thrown off the country's back in some great reassertion of the public will. As Prime Minister Trudeau said, virtually the only tool in the hands of Ottawa or Quebec City to perform that kind of extraordinary function was the blunt instrument of War Measures. As the panic mounted and the pressure from Quebec increased, Mr. Trudeau finally chose to accede to it.

From this perspective, it is not an important question to ask what kind of secret information fed the governments' apprehensions. What is most important is to judge whether the model used by Ottawa and Quebec City to interpret the unfolding situation was a credible one, and to assess the results of the model's application.

The picture of events offered by Canada's political leaders was painted in bold strokes and shocking colours. It was intended to startle the public, and it did so. The prime minister said in his television address on October 16 that "there are very few times in the history of any country when all persons must take a stand on critical issues. This is one of those times; this is one of those issues."[32] He did not mean that there was a wide range of positions to be taken on the affair; he meant that there were two positions—either with the government in its tough-

ness, or against it with the bleeding hearts, the confused, the
terrorists and their supporters. He did not conceal that he
hoped to force Canadians to choose sides simply in the affair,
and he did not hide his impression, later, that this choice would
have lasting influences upon the evolution of the Quebec nationalist movement.[33]

What he was asking for was public acceptance of the official
model of events. The unusual prophecies or near-prophecies
made by Mr. Drapeau, Mr. Bourassa and Mr. Marchand
about a wave of assassinations, dynamitings in Montreal, a
coup d'état in Quebec City, and the separation of Quebec from
Canada, while uttered in the heat of the moment, were all
coherent parts of the official model, and it would have meant
little for anyone to reject any particular prophecy made within
the pattern. A hundred other perfervid details might have been
added by anyone with a vivid political imagination. It was the
general conception which governed Ottawa's response. From
the viewpoint of a critic, such apparently farfetched assertions
about what was going to happen might appear dishonest, intimidating or fantastic; to someone who accepted the framework of interpretation, they were quite believable projections
of possibilities to be taken into account. And to those who
accepted the model, the actual consequences of Ottawa's harsh
response were by themselves insignificant; those consequences,
for example, involved the fates of James Cross and Pierre Laporte, the reputations of Claude Ryan and many dissenting
union, cultural and intellectual leaders, and the shaken possibility of maintaining the democratic process in Quebec.

Was Ottawa's interpretation of events reliable? One test of its
soundness is to consider whether the account given by the
country's leaders of what was actually happening in the crisis
was precise—or careless—in its details and intimations. The
problem of assessment is not to try to judge the accuracy of all
the speculations like those of the minister of regional economic
expansion, Mr. Marchand, or Mayor Drapeau, about what
might have happened but in fact did not; as John Turner said,

to suggest, as some members of the opposition have, that

because an insurrection did not occur, therefore it could not have been apprehended, is an exercise in false logic.[34]

The wilder hypotheses cannot be dealt with; they fit a theory of conspiracy but remain speculation.[35] The problem is rather to consider what claims of "fact" were offered in explanation of the need for War Measures, and to make the same kind of subjective judgment as did the federal cabinet about the reliability of this information and its implications. If a case is justified with accurate evidence, there is some reason to take it seriously; if it is not, there is good ground for scepticism. Some reasons to doubt the authorities' judgment of events have been suggested previously; a more general analysis is now appropriate.

For this purpose, Prime Minister Trudeau's television address of October 16 is a central element.[36] This speech was the first formal attempt by the prime minister, and it remains his only extensive attempt, to speak to the Canadian public about what was happening. It offered somewhat more general comments about Quebec, the FLQ, and the responsibilities of government than either Mr. Trudeau or Mr. Turner had made in the House of Commons earlier in the day. It was a major effort in persuasion. The address was emotionally powerful, a result of its presentation and content as well as of the drama of the situation. Mr. Trudeau sat almost motionless at his desk, his face impassive throughout; but he conveyed the sense of an implacable will and a relentless anger through slight shifts of intonation and an icy stare that shot out at moments from frigid depths. This was a formidable man. Set against the disorderly passion of Robert Lemieux's press conferences and the anxious television commentaries on events in the previous days, the prime minister's display of controlled passion was masterly and hypnotic. It was a brilliant performance, and it succeeded overwhelmingly as advocacy. As rational argument, however, it was a demagogic display of charged language, clever device, undefended assertion, and questionable psychology. Some parts of the speech require most careful reconsideration.

The prime minister insisted at three points that terrorist kidnappings could occur anywhere in Canada and could have any victims. "To the kidnappers," he insisted, "their identity is immaterial;" the hostages might easily be "you or me, or perhaps some child" or "innocent members of your family or of your neighbourhood." This was smudging the evidence, and its intention could only be to alarm the national audience into uncritical support for a harsh official policy. The claim that the violence could equally well have occurred outside Quebec was a bizarre variation on the federalist theme that Quebec is a province like the others. It ignored the obvious evidence that the FLQ is a Quebec terrorist organization concerned with Quebec objectives, and that the province had a seven-year record of terrorist activities not experienced by any other part of the country. To admit this is not to express some kind of judgment upon Quebec, but to recognize facts. There is more present danger of terror in Montreal than in Toronto or Medicine Hat, and to claim that this is not so is careless or irresponsible or cynically misleading. But the point was repeated and repeated.

The claim that the victims could be any persons in Canada is equally misleading. Aside from the case of the Palestinian jet hijackings, there has been an entirely consistent pattern to recent terrorist kidnappings. The victims have been, exclusively, diplomats and politicians. This cannot be reassuring to such persons, but it is elementary to recognize the fact, and it is gratuitous and dishonest to deny it. Mr. Trudeau's government admitted this by implication when it assigned police and military guards to—precisely—diplomats, leading politicians and senior civil servants, and not to ordinary citizens. It admits the fact again when it considers the creation of a special protection service for diplomats serving in Canada.[37] Marighella's *Minimanual for the Urban Guerrilla* limits the targets of political kidnapping to members of the police or police spies, political leaders, or "notorious and dangerous enem[ies] of the revolutionary movement." It warns that other prominent persons who have no "political interest" should only be the victims of kidnapping in exceptional cases:

The kidnapping of personalities who . . . are outstanding

in some other field . . . can be a useful form of propaganda for the revolutionary and patriotic principles of the urban guerrilla, provided it occurs under special circumstances, and the kidnapping is handled so that the public sympathizes with it and accepts it.[38]

When James Cross was asked his opinion of why he was chosen as a hostage, his reply was:

I think they wanted a diplomat. They had already tried three, two at least, and possibly three kidnapping attempts in Montreal, which had been frustrated. They had surveyed numbers of people. They gave me a few reasons when I asked them, claiming British cultural imperialism in Canada, but I don't believe this. I think they simply wanted a diplomat to get world opinion and I happened to be available.[39]

The statement that was purported to have been made by Francis Simard and introduced as evidence in the Laporte inquest said that:

In view of the developments in the Cross case, we formed the Chenier cell and decided to kidnap Pierre Laporte. We wanted to delay the execution of Cross, who was not responsible for Quebec's problems.[40]

They chose Mr. Laporte, apparently, because they felt he *was* responsible. (Pierre Vallières, the FLQ propagandist, had described him, along with Jean Drapeau and Daniel Johnson, as "the most cunning of the leaders of the Right.")[41] Another member of the kidnapping cell, Bernard Lortie, testified to the Laporte inquest that "since Cross did not make the ruling authorities move, we decided to kidnap Mr. Laporte."[42]

None of these statements suggests that the identity of the hostages was immaterial; on the contrary, it was a crucial part of the terrorist plan. It was the prominence of the victims, and their closeness to the centres of power repudiated by the terrorists, that made them potential hostages. The sense of security of the political leadership, not of the common citizens of Quebec, was being directly challenged. Why, then, should the prime minister try to generalize the danger of kidnapping?

Mr. Trudeau's account of the terrorists' demands, too, was either sloppy or disingenuous. He spoke as though there had been no willingness to compromise shown in ten days of terrorist messages, as though the original statement of demands had been final. The revolutionaries, he said, threatened "to murder in cold blood two innocent men unless their demands are met." What, then, of the assurance that Mr. Cross's life would not depend upon the refusal to pay ransom?[43] Or the declaration in the final note of October 12 that Mr. Cross would be freed, and the threat to Mr. Laporte's life suspended, upon liberation of the prisoners and suspension of the police searches?[44] When he came to listing the kidnappers' demands, the prime minister mentioned them in this order: first, "they want their grievances aired by force in public"; second, "they want the police to offer up as a sacrificial lamb a person whom they assume assisted in the lawful arrest and proper conviction of certain of their criminal friends"; third, "they also want money. Ransom money"; and finally he came to the central demand for the release of prisoners.

This exposition was tendentious and incorrect. Mr. Trudeau did not mention that his government had already, eight days before, conceded the demand that the FLQ manifesto be read over the CBC French-language network; nor that the FLQ had implicitly abandoned its demands for ransom money and delivery of the name of the informer. There was remarkable insensitivity to the situation in this account; and once again the predictable result was to heighten public fear and outrage rather than to offer his listeners material for calm judgment of the crisis. Fear and outrage were presumably considered to be the responses that would lead the public to support War Measures uncritically.

Finally, there was a series of assertions in the speech about the nature and objectives of the FLQ, and the consequences of appeasing terror, which are open to serious doubt. The kidnappers were "men who are attempting to destroy the unity and the freedom of Canada." They were "a handful of self-selected dictators;" and "those who gain power through terror, rule through terror." Surrender to the FLQ's demands, the prime minister said (giving the highest stamp of authority to the conventional theory), would bring increased terrorist activity in Quebec, would invite terrorism across the country, would result in "the breakdown of the legal system, and its replacement by the law of the jungle." On the contrary, "if we stand firm, this current situation will soon pass." The hope was raised that the use of emergency measures would effectively "root out the cancer of an armed, revolutionary movement."

The two sets of alternatives were presented with Manichean simplicity, and starkly, as axioms that required no evidence for their support. Here we are slipping into the realm of the hypothetical, where the analysis of sweeping language can easily be as careless as the language itself. But the prime minister's claims are susceptible to some testing against whatever evidence there is of the FLQ's intentions, and against the evidence of terrorist psychology in general.

The prime minister was aware, intellectually, of the dangers of his stance. He warned that

> this extreme position into which governments have been forced is in some respects a trap. It is a well-known technique of revolutionary groups who attempt to destroy society by unjustified violence to goad the authorities into inflexible attitudes.

He was aware, but it made no difference to his choice. He asked merely that the public should remember that it was the terrorists who made the opening play in "this vicious game." That is a fair request. But it doesn't get us far. We can remember and condemn the terrorists; but we are left, nevertheless, playing the game on the terrorists' ruthless terms.

Twenty-four hours later they made their next play in response to War Measures and the end of negotiations. On Saturday evening, October 17, the recovery of the body of Pierre Laporte at St. Hubert airport, strangled and dumped in the trunk of an abandoned car, confirmed that it was indeed a vicious game.

4: "Have these gentlemen ever seen a revolution?"

In responding as they did to terror, the Quebec government and the Canadian government ignored the record and the lessons of an earlier period of European terrorism. Vague references to Kerensky's Russia and Weimar Germany were offered by Mr. Trudeau and Mr. Turner as warnings to the public of what fates befall countries unprepared to defend themselves against the revolutionary seizure of power. But the analogies were inappropriate. Quebec was not confronted in 1970 with the kind of challenge to the constitutional order made by the Bolshevik party in Russia or by the Nazi party in Germany. The first was a highly disciplined, professional revolutionary conspiracy, aimed at establishing a rigid system of centralized control; the other was a right-wing mass party supported by a large private army which came to power through the use and misuse of the regular electoral machinery. The Front de Libération du Québec, in contrast, is a loose, leaderless and fluid association of semi-independent cells, without the capacity or the coherent ambition to seize political power for itself. This does not mean that the FLQ can be ignored, but only that we must search elsewhere for historical parallels which may offer some guidance in understanding and reacting to its peculiar challenge.

At one point in his speech to the House of October 16, Prime Minister Trudeau said that he was dealing with a type of person "who in earlier times would have been desribed as an anarchist;" but this fleeting revelation drifted away in the confusion. In their acts, the governments disregarded the implications of the prime minister's remark. The statement may, in fact, have been intended to confuse rather than to enlighten the public, for it played upon the popular fear of anarchy as the triumph of disorder, of anarchists as hooded, bomb-throwing nihilists who wish only to destroy. In his earlier writings, Mr. Trudeau normally used the word 'anarchy' as a pejorative synonym for complete social disorder. (George Woodcock has accused Pierre Trudeau of "a demagogy unworthy of a political scientist" in speaking of the FLQ as anarchist, and Pierre Vallières himself condemns those in Quebec who talk of FLQ members as "irresponsible and dangerous 'anarchists.' ")[1]

But anarchism deserves better than to be reduced to or equated with mindless violence, and the fact that the word is commonly used in this way—and thus considered with horror —obscures our comprehension of the FLQ. The pattern is of course not entirely consistent, but there is strong evidence—in the FLQ's declarations of aims, its organization and methods of action, its membership, and its ties with the broader community—of a family relationship with previous movements of anarchist terrorism.[2] At this stage in its evolution, the FLQ can be most clearly understood if it is seen in this way. If Mr. Trudeau had pursued his insight, the governments might have made a fundamentally different response to the terror.

Anarchism is not just an outdated creed "of earlier times"; it is a reflection of certain human needs and frustrations as evident in mid-twentieth century Quebec as in nineteenth century Spain, and traceable far back into the millenarian religious movements of the Middle Ages. The anarchists, says James Joll,

> have attacked, often in the most brutal and direct manner, the values and institutions of the established social and moral order. Much of this has ended in futility, sometimes farcical, sometimes tragic. Yet the protests which the anarchist movement has made express a recurrent psycholog-

ical need, and one which has by no means disappeared
with the apparent failure of anarchism as a serious social
and political force.[3]

Modern anarchism and its terrorist variation are products of
the disruption caused to traditional agricultural and artisan
communities by the creation of an industrial society, by the
hopes of progress and the disappointing reality experienced by
many persons caught up in the industrial order. (Anarchism
shares the ground, as a consequence of this historic transition,
with nineteenth century socialism and conservatism. All three
reflect a distaste for materialism and specialization, a suspicion
of technology, a desire for "community," and a language of
protest against liberal, bourgeois society. And yet anarchism, in
some respects, is also a kind of liberal fundamentalism, seeking
the achievement of individual liberty against the centralizing,
liberal economic and political systems of the age.)[4]

Modern capitalist industry, and the administrative and political institutions which have grown along with it, have created in the societies of the western world a large and complacent middle class. But as we have become increasingly aware,
this relatively privileged middle class has been offset by another loosely defined class that has failed to come satisfactorily to
terms with the insistent disciplines, bureaucratic rigidities, im-
personality, and indignity of the industrial system: which, indeed, has been exploited and degraded by the system. Some of
those uprooted from the security of life in the village and the
family over the past two centuries have found it impossible to
root themselves with any material security and moral comfort
in the modern world. Others with temporary security in the
system have found this security suddenly and irrationally removed. Anarchism, in its nineteenth century evolution, reflected strongly these experiences of indignity and uprootedness in
the newly industrializing countries of continental Europe (and
among European immigrants in the United States). Its spokesmen reflected back nostalgically to the communal warmth and
autonomy of small, rural societies, condemning modern life
from that humane perspective.

There were, on one side, vicious indignities and disappoint-ments for many Europeans as society lurched into the liberal individualist age of the factory and mass production system; and there were, in contrast, the universal hopes raised by the mythology of the French revolution and the Enlightenment. The gulf between utopian hopes and present despair led some men to challenge fundamentally the entire social, political and economic system; it led others, encouraged by this critical anal-ysis, to desperate acts of violence aimed at bringing down the iniquitous social and political systems and installing the perfect society of independent men. The same gulf between promise and reality, the same insecurities in a time of retarded but now rapid social change have brought the same analysis and the same kinds of desperate acts in Quebec since 1963. The familiar alienation from the industrial system is intensified in Quebec by the fact that this system is also colonial, largely owned outside the province and managed in another language.[5]

The analogy to the present situation which deserves our study is that of the wave of anarchist terror which swept west-ern Europe and touched the United States in the period from the assassination of Tsar Alexander II of Russia in 1881 to the death of Archduke Francis Ferdinand at Sarajevo in 1914. Af-ter an interval of half a century, a new cycle of disruption and terror which finds its justification in an articulately anarchist ideology has begun in western Europe, Latin America and now in Canada. In the long view, this can be seen as one further episode in a single historic movement against the pervasive dominance of industry, technology and liberal capitalism in the modern world.

Irving Kristol considers the difficulty of understanding con-temporary radical movements to be the result of an intentional mystification of events:

> When we lack the will to see things as they really are, there is nothing so mystifying as the obvious. This is the case, I think, with the new upsurge of radicalism that is now shaking much of Western society to its foundations. We have constructed the most ingenious sociological and psy-

chological theories—as well as a few disingenuously naive ones—to explain this phenomenon. But there is in truth no mystery here. Our youthful rebels are anything but inarticulate; and though they utter a great deal of nonsense, the import of what they are saying is clear enough. What they are saying is that they dislike—to put it mildly—the liberal, individualist, capitalist civilization that stands ready to receive them as citizens. They are rejecting this offer of citizenship and are declaring their desire to see some other kind of civilization replace it.[6]

Or they are demanding that it live up to its libertarian pretensions. From well before the moment in May, 1968, when the black flag was defiantly hoisted from the roof of the Odéon Theatre in Paris by dissenting students of the Sorbonne until the kidnapping of Pierre Laporte in October, 1970, there has been a significant anarchist element in this new wave of rejected citizenship.

The nineteenth century anarchist movement entered its period of terrorism or "propaganda by the deed" after its failure to attract massive working class support and as a reflection of bitterness over the severity of police repression. The turn to violence in the 1880s and 1890s was a reflection of despair and frustration, not of confidence in the movement. Gerald Brenan writes:

The reign of the bourgeoisie was now at its height. Their meanness, their philistinism, their insufferable self-righteousness weighed upon everything. They had created a world that was both dull and ugly and they were so firmly established in it that it seemed hopeless even to dream of revolution. The desire to shake by some violent action the complacency of this huge, inert and stagnant mass of middle-class opinion became irresistible. One must put such books as Flaubert's *Bouvard et Pécuchet* and Huysmans' *A Rebours*, Butler's and Wilde's epigrams and Nietzche's savage outbursts in the same category as the bombs of the Anarchists. To shock, to infuriate, to register one's protest became the only thing that any decent or sensitive man could do.[7]

The anarchist prophet, Michael Bakunin, hoped that his revolution would be made by the mass of despondent peasantry and the poorest urban proletariat of the primitively industrial areas: not by the moderately prosperous urban workers, whom he expected to join the middle class. But his movement would, he expected, be led by men who had freed themselves from the *lumpenproletariat*,

> young men down from the universities who could not find jobs, school teachers, petit bourgeois, déclassés who 'whether they know it or not belong to the Revolution.'[8]

And such persons were in fact the terrorist leaders in Russia, Italy and Spain in the 1880s and 1890s—as they are today in Quebec. Bakunin hoped, but hoped in vain, that the violent acts of this revolutionary core would prompt widespread strikes and public disturbances, until a general rising would finally sweep away all public institutions. The small groups of subversives sprang into existence as Bakunin had expected they would; but what was notable about the terrorist waves of the 1880s and 1890s was that they uniformly failed in their major objective: they did not overthrow the institutions of the state. Anarchist terrorism was a movement of failure, negative and protestant at its heart, conditioned not to triumph but increasingly to defeat. It was a theatrical movement of gesture and act which fed upon the immediate satisfactions of the deed rather than upon any realistic hope of transforming society.

This paradox arose from the libertarian objectives of the movement. The goal was not the establishment of a revolutionary state, disciplined and centralized, but the destruction of all institutional authority. The movement itself, therefore, was anarchic in its non-organization. It had no central leadership, it imposed no discipline, it issued no commands. It could not sustain prolonged and systematic revolt, and it offered no leaders ready to seize the instruments of power. Its dynamics were the sensation of the vicious act itself and—once a cycle of terrorism had begun—the desire for revenge, the spur to further terror offered by the repressive and often indiscriminate responses of the authorities.

Friedrich Engels looked upon the futility of anarchist revolutionary action with contempt.

> They demand that the first act of the social revolution shall be the abolition of authority. Have these gentlemen ever seen a revolution? A revolution is certainly the most authoritarian thing there is: it is the act whereby one part of the population imposes its will on the other part by means of rifles, bayonets and cannon—authoritative means if such there be at all; and if the victorious party does not wish to have fought in vain, it must maintain this rule by means of the terror which its arms inspire in the reactionaries.[9]

And James Joll remarks that "the tragedy of the revolutionary movement has been that Engels was right . . . those revolutionaries, such as the anarchists in the Spanish Civil War, who have put Bakunin's organizational doctrines into practice, have failed to survive."[10]

When Prime Minister Trudeau said that "those who gain power through terror, rule through terror," he was taking Engels' side in the controversy about revolutionary power. But he was inaccurate on two counts. It is not necessarily true that terrorist rule follows the terrorist seizure of power; many other circumstances, including the balance of power among the various groups in the revolutionary movement, the character of individual leaders, and the particular political tradition of the nation concerned, will affect the outcome. The Irish Republic, Israel and Kenya came into existence in this century as independent states following prolonged terrorism and violence. But they are hardly the examples of rule through terror that Mr. Trudeau spoke of. His statement is far too sweeping in its condemnation of revolutionary movements, far too careless to be a perceptive comment upon the possibilities for Quebec society.

What is more, the prime minister's statement takes for granted a disciplined and systematic attempt on the part of the FLQ to seize power in Quebec. But having learned of the pathetic surrender of three members of the Chenier cell as they struggled up from their hole in the ground with a shotgun and a starter's pistol, can we now believe that they seriously expected to overthrow the Quebec government? Even if, in moments of romantic madness, they actually did expect it, was the prospect real? On the contrary, the words and acts of the FLQ suggest that the movement is, at this stage (whether entirely consciously or not), anarchist in its approach, and doomed to the futility of anarchist terror.

The prime minister spoke of the FLQ as a "parallel power" and as "a handful of self-selected dictators" seeking power through terror; and other spokesmen for the official position also argued that the group sought to overthrow the state and install a revolutionary dictatorship.[11] The FLQ is certainly a "revolutionary" organization; but there are revolutionaries and revolutionaries. There is nothing in the public declarations and manifestos of the association to support the claim that the FLQ seeks or has any practical chance of forming a new revolutionary administration in Quebec.

As the FLQ has gradually articulated its assumptions and objectives since 1963, its message has become increasingly anarchist in tone and content. The first manifesto, a "Notice to the Population of the State of Quebec" issued in March, 1963, following the first series of fire-bombings of Canadian Army buildings in Montreal, declared that the FLQ "is a revolutionary movement of volunteers ready to die for the political and economic independence of Quebec."[12] The manifesto spoke of FLQ members as "suicide-commandos" whose purpose was "the complete destruction" by sabotage of

a) all colonial (federal) symbols and institutions, in particular the RCMP and the armed forces;
b) all the information media in the colonial language (English) which hold us in contempt;
c) all commercial establishments and enterprises which

    practise discrimination against Quebecers, which do not
    use French as the first language, which advertise in the
    colonial language (English);
  d) all plants and factories which discriminate against
    French-speaking workers.

In addition, said the declaration, the FLQ "will also attack
all American cultural and commercial interests, natural allies of
English colonialism." The peroration announced in ringing language that

> The dignity of the Quebec people demands independence.
> Quebec's independence is only possible through social rev-
> olution.
> Social revolution means a free Quebec.
> Students, workers, peasants, form your clandestine groups
> against Anglo-American colonialism.

The claims reflected and appealed to a spirit of anger and
humiliation; the promises of destruction were grandiose; and
there was nothing in the document to suggest that thought had
been given by its drafters to the kind of state that would follow
the revolution, except that it would be "free."

The FLQ pamphlet of 1969, "Revolutionary Strategy and
the Role of the Avant-Garde," which was presented in evidence
by the Montreal civic administration to the House of Commons committee examining subversion within the Company of
Young Canadians, was sharper in its focus.[13]

> The strategic objective is clear to all: the destruction of the
> capitalist society and the construction of an egalitarian,
> just and free society founded on the practice of collective
> self-determination at all levels (economic, administrative,
> scholastic, and cultural).

The FLQ, said the document, did not aim to command or to
replace the unions and citizens' committees, but only "to fur-
nish them with the political and ideological weapons they need,
not only to confront the bourgeois system, but above all to

destroy it." The FLQ foresaw, in conventional anarchist terms and arising from its own inspiration, the growth of mass popular insurrection leading to an egalitarian society. The statement came close to an explicit rejection of the Communist pattern of the party as a disciplined revolutionary vanguard which would take power itself:

> To achieve this [egalitarian society] we must shed the bad habit of using the movements of Marx, Lenin, Mao Tse-Tung and Castro as ready-made models of revolutionary organizations ... To us, these revolutionary theories serve more as methods to adapt to our own national reality, rather than as models. . . .

The emphasis, instead, was upon the exemplary role of the FLQ and the autonomy of local anti-capitalist committees. Even the English-speaking population and the federal system had disappeared as major targets, to be replaced by bourgeois society and the capitalist economic system. This document echoed in a simplified way the libertarian and egalitarian tone of Pierre Vallières' *Nègres blancs d'Amérique*, which was first published in 1968 and rapidly gained its reputation as the handbook of the FLQ.

The book offers rather confused tactical guidance to Quebec revolutionaries. Vallières sees the revolutionary process as a long one, leading eventually to "the organization of a true revolutionary army capable of defeating imperialism." On one page he deplores spontaneous individual acts of violence, while on the next he advocates them as necessary steps in a mounting campaign of disruption.[14] He explicitly disavows anarchist revolt as impractical because it rejects systematic organization, but nevertheless sets the final goal of revolution as a utopian anarchist community. The over-all purpose of his analysis in *White Niggers of America* is to create general commitment to the anarchist goal, and therefore to the revolutionary acts that will lead to its creation. His relativism allows him to be tactically very flexible; his scheme is open enough to accommodate different kinds of acts and organization at different stages.

When the kidnappings occurred in October, 1970, the Liberation cell insisted that a new and more comprehensive manifesto be broadcast to Quebec, which declared:

> The Front de Libération du Québec wants the total independence of Quebecers, united in a free society, purged forever of the clique of voracious sharks, the patronizing "big bosses" and their henchmen who have made Quebec their hunting preserve for "cheap labour" and unscrupulous exploitation ...
>
> Workers of Quebec, start today to take back what is yours; take for yourselves what belongs to you. Only you know your factories, your machines, your hotels, your universities, your unions. Don't wait for an organizational miracle.
>
> Make your own revolution in your areas, in your places of work. . . . Only you are able to build a free society.
>
> We must fight, not one by one, but together. We must fight until victory is ours with all the means at our disposal as did the patriots of 1837-38 ...
>
> We are the workers of Quebec and we will go on to the end. We want to replace the slave society with a free society, functioning by itself and for itself. An open society to the world.[15]

The language is not new. It is not the language of Lenin, but of Proudhon and Bakunin, the enemies of all power. It is not authoritarian but libertarian, seeking not tyranny but the free community of equal men, subservient to no one. The manifesto exalts the individual man, free of the restraints imposed upon him by the centralized state, by capitalism and industrialism, and by the church: all of them, in anarchist eyes, the instruments of modern oppression. The words and the targets of scorn are in the classic anarchist mould. Farga Pellicer, the Spanish anarchist who declared in 1870 that "we wish the rule of Capital, State and Church to cease and to construct upon their ruins Anarchy, the free federation of free associations of free workers,"[16] would have been at home with the manifesto writers of the FLQ.

The words of the manifesto, like those of Bakunin and his followers of eighty years ago, indicate the kind of vision that sustains and moves the most persistent of the terrorists. It is easy to describe them as bandits and criminals and vicious men, but it deprives us of understanding. This language of contempt suggests that they are less than human, that they lack the normal sentiments of civilized men, that they are simply brutal and unfeeling. Obviously a terrorist must harden himself in order to commit violence; but anarchist terror has a deeper foundation than mere viciousness. It rests upon a conviction of righteousness, a fanatic idealism and a generous belief in the capacity of men to govern themselves without the imposition of external authority. It is a humane and naive faith, which can easily be clung to by psychopaths seeking private vengeance; but it is not at its core a faith of heartless men.[17]

Pierre Vallières sees the goal of the Quebec revolution as the elimination of the oppressive institutions of capitalism and the state, and the liberation of ordinary men "to fulfill themselves as persons, through fraternity, love, solidarity. ... "[18] If we fail to take notice of this evidence of humanity in the terrorists, we are likely to underestimate the depth of their commitment and to misjudge their purposes. They too, like most men, must believe that what they are doing is right and serves a human purpose; and that belief sustains them. Anarchist utopianism has its aspect of nobility, and recourse to that nobility can override for the terrorist the vileness of the acts he is pledged to commit. The belief keeps him sane and masks his despair. Other men may disagree profoundly with the terrorists and be repelled by their acts; but the terrorists should not be denied their humanity. One result of doing that will be to countenance the disregard of their civil rights: for what does it matter, if such beings are not really human? But every occasion of this kind of disregard offers more justifiable evidence to the disenchanted of the iniquity of the system. The ordinary norms and procedures of the criminal law must be applied to the terrorists as to other offenders; the sloppy attribution to them of a general quality of inhumanity is mistaken and unjustifiable.

The proclamations of modern anarchism arouse hopes of the millenium; they are meant to quicken the faith. They say little about the seizure of power, but speak instead of its destruction and its replacement with a simplified and more humane order. They offer few precise clues to the kind of constitution that will exist after the collapse of authority, except that it will be freer than man has ever hoped or known. Anarchists do not seek, like Leninist revolutionaries, to seize the mechanisms of the state for themselves, since they reject the very conception of centralized power. This may be novel and difficult for conventional politicians, themselves participants in the competition for power, to believe; but it is the central and persistent element of anarchist belief and cannot simply be denied.

The FLQ is moved by this utopian faith. The organization seems to lack any permanent core of leaders who might form the nucleus of a successful revolutionary regime, and the semi-autonomous cells seem to have no concern for such leadership. The human capacity to seize power does not exist in the FLQ; and the possibility that there was a serious threat to authority from the FLQ itself is the purest fantasy. As Gérard Pelletier admitted in March, 1971:

> I am perplexed by the hypothesis of a central leadership of the FLQ, a sort of grey eminence pulling the strings from afar. I also hesitate to believe in a plan or in a strategic coordination of the various FLQ cells.[19]

The waves of anarchist terror at the end of the nineteenth century followed the pattern of epidemics. Examples of violence were infectious, and the infection was international. National boundaries offered no constraints; where the social circumstances were sufficiently similar, terror once begun was repeated. There was an internal dynamic to such outbursts, a certain psychological necessity that they should proceed from violent act to violent act, each bolder and more repulsive than the last, until finally the overindulgence in violence exhausted the moral energy of the participants and repelled the general population with its futility. Then the epidemics died.[20]

To the very limited extent that the state's response affected the terrorist compulsion, the evidence suggests that acts of defiance or severe repression by the authorities stimulated rather than suppressed the terror. Many bomb attacks in France and Spain in the 1890s were justified by their agents as specific acts of revenge for excessive or indiscriminate punishments imposed for earlier acts of terror.[21]

Both these aspects of terrorist psychology, the self-sustaining element and the element of revenge, indicate the extremely limited ability of the state to influence anarchist terrorism in ways which will help directly to eliminate it. One bold act emboldens other potential terrorists, whether or not they have any personal association with the first terrorists. The act stimulates a desire in other men to prove themselves as extreme as, or more extreme than, the original agents. This desire for emulation works largely independently of the "success" or "failure" of the terrorists in achieving their longer range aims—such as the actual destruction of civic institutions or the satisfaction of ransom demands. It is the deed itself—the bomb explosion, the kidnapping, the murder—which rivets attention and demands repetition. The international epidemic of bombings, political kidnappings and aircraft hijackings since 1968 seems to have followed this kind of self-perpetuating momentum. In some cases demands have been resisted while in others they have been met, but neither response has been clearly effective in halting repeated imitations. What can be asserted is that political terrorists require immediate pretexts as well as theoretical goals to rationalize their acts, and if governments deny them those pretexts by displaying willingness to satisfy their humane demands, or by refusing to indulge in careless repression, the terrorists are left with no justification to proceed.

Whenever governments since 1968 have liberated "political prisoners" in response to kidnappers' demands, the kidnappers have released their hostages. But when governments have resisted the demands, lives have been lost and further acts of terror have not been prevented. The Canadian government's refusal to meet the basic demand of the FLQ for the release of prisoners is unlikely, from this perspective, to have the desired effect on the future behaviour of the terrorists; but it did amount to a challenge to the FLQ to carry out its murder threat, and one cell accepted the challenge.

The spontaneity of anarchist acts and the absence of central leadership deny to such movements the possibility of overthrowing the state; and this means that the authorities should not overestimate the general danger from anarchist terror. On the other hand, this kind of movement tends to be unusually resilient: the FLQ has sufficiently demonstrated that quality in its eight-year history. The disconnected and informal cellular organization of the FLQ provides it with the same flexibility and means of resisting repression as proved so durable in European anarchist organizations. Gerald Brenan says of the Spanish movement of the 1890s that

> at moments of enthusiasm, the number of workers controlled by the Anarchists would double and treble themselves and, when the inevitable reaction came, would shrink back to a small kernel of convinced militants. This plasticity of the Anarchist movement enabled it to survive persecutions and, as soon as they were over, to reappear stronger than ever.[22]

This kind of strength is resistant to the most efficient police action, for the organization literally fades away when the pressure is applied. Any attempt to estimate the number of militants, or to judge the seriousness of the challenge or the success of police action according to such an estimate, becomes futile and even ludicrous. In the active phase there may be few or many militants, depending on the momentary atmosphere. The police and the bureaucracies, being inclined to reassure themselves with hard statistics, may resist this precautionary conclusion. But if they do, they will continue to make the same misjudgments about the movement that they have in the past, when announcements were periodically made that it had been successfully eliminated. Humiliating proof that such boasts are false (in the form of further rounds of terror) may then have the dangerous effect of driving the frustrated authorities into more and more imprudent acts of repression.

The ability of such an organization to dissolve into the community around it indicates something vital about that community. Anarchist terrorism can only persist for any length of time in a social atmosphere that tolerates it. The seven-year history of mounting terror by the FLQ is enough to indicate that the FLQ is not an alien infection, a "cancer" to be rooted out of the body politic by the administration of some kind of determined surgery or bitter political medicine. It is, rather, one manifestation of deep and widespread human frustrations in Quebec society, which are felt by far more persons than those few who actively associate themselves with the FLQ. The declarations and impudent acts of the terrorists speak to the complacent part of the community, and to the politicians, of the depth of these frustrations; and those silent, passive, beaten citizens who cannot speak for themselves recognize their own voices in such acts. Terrorism, thus, can be a source of pride and a means of restoring dignity to the disinherited; it vividly asserts a will which these persons scarcely know they possess. As Ann Charney wrote of the October events:

> Whatever feelings they had about the FLQ and its methods, many French Quebeckers could not help feeling some thrill as the humbled flag of a suppressed revolt [of 1837] was resuscitated and splashed across the pages of every newspaper in Canada. In the same way, the names of the FLQ cells, and the language of their communiques, emphasized many aspects of the past, which traditional histories had intentionally left out. The extent of such reawakened pride is hard to gauge. There was no organized, official way in which it could express itself at that time. Indications of it, however, were frequently evident in conversations with friends and neighbours.[23]

And if men's self-respect is touched and momentarily strength-

ened by acts of terror, they will not be inclined to offer their
wholehearted support to the police in their efforts to track
down the terrorist organization.

The resistance to police activity need not be, and is unlikely
to be, an active resistance. If it is passive, that is sufficient
reassurance and aid to the terrorists. It is enough for those who
have somehow crossed paths with the extremists, or those who
might possibly do so, to close their eyes at appropriate times,
and to take the view that investigation is the task of the police
alone, without active help from the community. A decision on
the part of many people to suspend judgment, to keep out of
the crisis, and to keep their eyes and mouths closed, serves
both as a sign of support for the terrorists and an efficient
means of complicating police work. Marighella instructs urban terrorists that:

> It is enough to win the support of a part of the people and
> this can be done by popularizing the following slogan: "let
> he [*sic*] who does not wish to do anything for the revolu-
> tionaries do nothing against them."[24]

Pierre Vallières was confident enough of widespread toleration
for the FLQ to write in 1969 that

> the more relentlessly the established Order pursues the
> FLQ, the more the FLQ's prestige increases and the more
> its influence spreads, especially among the most disadvan-
> taged, whom everything daily incites to armed rebellion. In
> vain do the authorities multiply rewards; the population
> does not collaborate with the police in the hunt for 'terror-
> ists.' . . . While the police waste time and the government
> grows impatient, the FLQ (which with each arrest the au-
> thorities consider to be definitely broken) constantly ex-
> pands its action.[25]

This was not just propagandist rhetoric: in October, 1970, the
judgment still seemed accurate. The fact that three members of
the FLQ Chenier cell remained at liberty, in four makeshift
hideouts and with the active help or knowledge of more than a

handful of persons, for over three months after the kidnapping
and murder of Pierre Laporte, indicates a fair degree of toleration. The successful custody of James Cross by the Liberation
cell in one house in north Montreal for two months, while the
kidnappers apparently continued to enter and leave the house
and to use local stores, offers even clearer evidence of sympathy for the movement.[26]

If this kind of passive support really does exist, as it seems to
in Montreal, the delicacy of a government's task in dealing
with terror (and at the same time maintaining an atmosphere of
democratic tolerance in the community) becomes still more obvious. Every word and every act of the authorities must be
carefully calculated (in their own interest) not to antagonize
and alienate further those who have a latent sympathy for the
terrorists, but instead to persuade them out of that sympathy.
Expressions or acts of contempt for the humanity and good
faith of the terrorists are likely to be imprudent for that reason
as well as others: such contempt will be taken as a general
insult to a whole section of society.

Another way of looking at the complicated relationship of
the FLQ to the community, and of assessing its moral strength,
is to consider the great variety of protest groups which have
offered havens to the terrorists in recent years. Most of the
faces of the kidnappers were familiar to the police because they
had been identified previously as participants in nationalist
street demonstrations, the McGill Français campaign, the
Mouvement pour la libération du taxi, the Mouvement pour
l'intégration scolaire, the Front de libération populaire, and the
Maison du pêcheur youth hostel in the Gaspé. During the
Quebec provincial election campaign of 1970, at least one of
the leading terrorists worked prominently as an organizer for
the Parti Québecois; other FLQ apologists were active in the
St. Henri Workers' Committee (a project supported by the
Company of Young Canadians) and in the Montreal civic election campaign of 1970 for the Front d'action politique. What
this indicates is not that these events and organizations were
"fronts" for the FLQ, or that most participants were themselves subversive or terrorists (as some politicians have irre-

sponsibly claimed), but that there were, before October, 1970, many sensitive targets of discontent in Quebec and many means of expressing that discontent. There was a whole range of tactical options open to those who sought social revolution or reform, a more responsive democracy, or national independence for Quebec, and events had not yet forced dissenters of varying degree to choose irrevocably among those options. It was the explicit policy of the FLQ, as long as this was possible, to engage in the whole range of extra-parliamentary political agitation, legal and public as well as clandestine.[27] Those who rejected terrorism as a legitimate or useful technique could still communicate with potential terrorists, and work alongside them in non-violent causes. In one sense the great diversity of activist causes outside the parliamentary system in Quebec represented an unusual and precarious instability in the political system; in another sense, that diversity was a source of reassurance to authority, because it offered safety valves for very explosive frustrations, and relatively peaceful warnings to politicians about what emotional demands had somehow to be satisfied. As long as non-violent activities continued to attract the interest of members of the FLQ, the danger of more brutal acts was marginally diminished.

Certainly some persons who worked most actively in the various non-violent campaigns did so in a desperate attempt to hold the potential terrorists within civilized limits. This difficult work of sanity involved a kind of collaboration and an unusual tolerance; but in Quebec before October it was natural and necessary. Through such associations, members of the FLQ came into fairly wide contact with other activist Quebecers, and probably reinforced the latent public toleration for the movement. The acts of October—of both the FLQ and the governments—have perhaps ended that fluid phase of public intermingling between the FLQ and other dissenting groups in the province. It is futile now to wish that that period could have been prolonged, or that it might have led to something else; but it is clear that Quebec and Canada are less civilized communities because of what followed.

What followed was the initial act of terror, an insensitive

official response, another act of terror, and the spread of hysteria among public officials sufficient to provoke a still cruder intervention by the state. Just as the governments misread the meaning of the acts of terror, they were also trapped by their own emotions in responding to terror. Yet the warnings of that danger, too, were clear in the European anarchist experience. For example, in the 1870s, as violence began to develop in Spain, ministers and members of the Cortes spoke wildly of the simple choice before Spaniards between "Don Carlos and Petrol," the monarchy or gasoline bombs, and warned of a vast international conspiracy financed by foreign gold and led by three hundred foreign agents.[28] The truth was that Bakunin could not pay his own railway fare to visit Barcelona, and the anarchist International could afford to send only two unpaid representatives to Spain who were missionaries rather than terrorists. Barbara Tuchman records the reaction of the city of Paris to one of the first terrorist bombings in the cycle of the 1890s:

> The city, wrote an English visitor, was "absolutely paralyzed" with fear. The upper classes "lived again as if in the days of the Commune. They dared not go to the theatres, to restaurants, to the fashionable shops in the Rue de la Paix or to ride in the Bois where Anarchists were suspected behind every tree." People exchanged terrible rumours: the Anarchists had mined the churches, poured prussic acid in the city's reservoirs, were hiding beneath the seats of horsecabs ready to spring out upon passengers and rob them. Troops were assembled in the suburbs ready to march, tourists took fright, the hotels were empty, buses ran without passengers, theatres and museums were barricaded.[29]

All because one man planted a bomb which exploded in a police station.

This kind of panic has been a characteristic response to sporadic terrorism in the western world for one hundred years. Such frightened rumour-mongering had its familiar parallel in

Montreal and among Quebec members of Parliament in October, 1970. Some members of the police forces "were so disconcerted . . . that they sent their wives and children away to the country, or even to other provinces."[30] Some MPs made almost hourly telephone calls from Ottawa to their Montreal homes during the week of October 12.[31] Conventions in Montreal were cancelled and the tourist trade fell off.[32] And Jean Marchand's apologia for War Measures in the House of Commons matched the wildest of French and Spanish speculations.[33] These illustrations were not evidence of any real danger of insurrection, as the panics following the European attacks of the last century were not; they were evidence of a quite general human readiness to be swept along at times in waves of mad rumour, uncertainty and fear. The human failing is understandable; it does not excuse the way in which the governments chose to appease it, first by silence, then by War Measures. In the entire period of ten days while the panic was mounting, the prime ministers of Canada and Quebec made no clear public efforts to calm the public anxiety with words; and their uncertain deeds prolonged and intensified it. Their joint indifference to the democratic leader's responsibility to promote public calm was one of the most stupid aspects of the crisis.

Mr. Trudeau and Mr. Bourassa need not have searched European history for guidance in dealing with public hysteria; they could have taken their lessons from Canadian experience. In 1919 the Winnipeg general strike was a minor event in an international ferment of discontent; and the result was Canada's version of the Red scare.

> Before the episode was concluded, the federal government had rushed through Parliament the infamous "Section 98" in amendment to the Criminal Code, by which a man could be found guilty of most serious offences on the weakest of evidence. This was a demonstration to many of how feeble the English tradition of freedom was when compared with the fears of the ruling classes: it weakened Canadian liberalism and many years were required before its repeal could be effected.[34]

But the only lesson the experience of 1919 offered the Canadian government in 1970 was that there was a ready-made statute to apply: so Section 98 came off the shelf and was transformed (with minor modification) into the Public Order Regulations, 1970.

In 1942 and after, under War Measures, the federal government conceded to a wave of entirely unsubstantiated panic in British Columbia to forcefully evict 21,000 persons of Japanese race (19,000 of them Canadian citizens) from the Pacific coast, seized their property, dispersed their communities, and subsequently deported nearly 4,000 persons to Japan. None of the victims was ever charged with any disloyal offence.[35]

What should have been learned from these events was that the real danger to a democratic society when panic arises is the state's readiness to appease that panic by disregarding civil liberties unjustly and unnecessarily. When Lester B. Pearson spoke to the House of Commons in the debate on the Canadian Bill of Rights in 1960, he said that he looked back upon the persecution of the Japanese Canadians with shame. Yet he believed that the action was taken "in complete good faith by a government which believed that it was essential at that time for the safety of our country, and in circumstances and in an atmosphere which it is easy to forget now." We have been reminded again of that kind of atmosphere. In retrospect, said Mr. Pearson, the Liberal party of Canada did "not believe that certain of those actions were really necessary, or that they should be repeated in any similar situation in the future."[36]

In Pierre Vallières' terms (as he spelled out the development of insurrection in *White Niggers of America*), the October acts of the FLQ were premature and inadequate to spark the revolution. Why then did they occur? Either the two FLQ cells were more anarchist than Vallières is, and prepared their plans without close attention to the warnings of the theoretician; or they understood his advice and in fact were not acting to create insurrection, but for some other more immediate purposes. The repertoire of the contemporary urban guerrilla movement is varied, and kidnapping has a special place in it. The *Minimanual for the Urban Guerrilla* defines the act:

Kidnapping is capturing and holding in a secret spot a police agent, a North American spy, a political personality, or a notorious and dangerous enemy of the revolutionary movement.

Kidnapping is used to exchange or liberate imprisoned revolutionary comrades, or to force suspension of torture in the jail cells of the military dictatorship.[37]

The words of the two FLQ cells should be taken at face value: they intended in October, 1970, to commit isolated acts of terror in order to frighten and test the authorities, and especially to seek the freedom of their associates in prison. In this view, the October acts were an anarchist preliminary stage or interlude of action in a revolutionary pattern which will not necessarily remain anarchist, but which is intended by the theorists of the movement to develop later into a disciplined, mass revolutionary movement. The governments of Quebec and Canada, by reading into events the immediate threat of a full-scale, blossoming insurrection, compressed the FLQ's own outline of long-term events into a short time-scale. This compression was an act of panic rather than of sound judgment. During the week of October 11-16 there was in fact very little evidence of the general collapse foreseen in the FLQ manifestos. The French-speaking Montreal public was "engaged" in the events, but only to the point of active curiosity. Apparently recognizing the precariousness of the situation and the danger to two lives, even the more militant among them showed great restraint. No major street demonstrations occurred, as they had many times in the previous two years; the rallies of sympathy for the FLQ sponsored by the CEGEPs and the Montreal universities were for contemporary Montreal, models of calm deliberation. Pierre Vallières and Charles Gagnon themselves successfully urged extreme discretion upon the student audience at Paul Sauvé Arena on the night of October 15, a few hours before the proclamation of War Measures.

The Trudeau government neglected this remarkable evidence of public restraint, and chose to act instead in response to pressure from the police, the Quebec and Montreal administrations, and frightened elements of the middle class population. This was not the noble act it seemed in English Canada. It was a slap in the face to democracy in Quebec, a condescending denial of the possibility that the Quebec public could respond maturely and soberly to the crisis, and could sustain its government in doing so. It was a paternal act of insensitivity reminiscent of the Duplessis regime, which also did not trust Quebec's democratic maturity. But in 1970 it was far more dangerous for authority to treat democracy with contempt than it had been ten years earlier. The "Declaration of the 'Sixteen'" made on Wednesday, October 14, put this point of view succinctly:

> We have reflected upon the fate of these two human lives, the collective reputation and honour of our society, and the real risk it is now running of social and political degradation. All these considerations make clear to us the fact that the primary responsibility for finding a solution and applying it must rest with Quebec. . . .
>
> This situation threatens to reduce Quebec and its government to a tragic impotence. We must make a superhuman effort to agree to negotiate and to compromise. On this level, we believe that Quebec and its government really have the moral mandate and the responsibility, the knowledge of the facts and of the political climate necessary to come to an informed decision.
>
> We feel this urgency all the more strongly because we fear, from certain quarters outside Quebec especially, the terrible temptation of embracing a political stance favouring the worst, i.e., the illusion that a chaotic and thoroughly ravaged Quebec would at last be easy to control, by any means whatever.[38]

5: Democracy, liberty and public order

How can the terrorists of October be fitted into our understanding of the Canadian democratic system? The rationalizations of those holding office in Montreal, Quebec City and Ottawa, which were used to justify the invocation of War Measures and its consequences, suggested that the commission of terrorist acts put the crisis outside the bounds of the normal democratic process. What did this claim imply about the authorities' understanding of democracy? Was that understanding adequate? If not, how would an adequate understanding have altered the response to terror?

The crucial points of concern are how the Canadian system permits the public will to be expressed, how clearly and immoveably the line is drawn between the legitimate and the illegitimate expression of dissent, and how the community allows itself to reply to acts of dissent which are considered to be beyond what is legitimate. The difficult question is not whether opposition or dissent should be permitted at all; democratic theory by definition allows for a range of legitimate dissent, and the opportunity to change governments by peaceful means according to established rules. Canadians are familiar with, and give every evidence of taking for granted, the normal right of opposition in the parliamentary system. The question is, what are the proper *limits* of dissent, what kind of opposition is not permissible—and why? And there are complementary questions: what are the proper limits of action which governments may take, first, against legitimate dissent, and second, against illegitimate dissent?

The three leaders chiefly responsible for the use of War Measures, Prime Minister Trudeau, Prime Minister Bourassa, and Mayor Drapeau, all seemed to understand that—given the extraordinary circumstances—their actions required justification in principle. Mr. Bourassa began his statement of October 11 with such a justification:

> The stability of our political institutions is menaced by events which are exceptional and unprecedented in our province. What makes these actions both fundamentally unjust and extremely dangerous is the fact that we live in a place where freedom of expression and action is one of the greatest of all the countries of the world.
>
> Even the political parties who question the political system itself have every liberty to express themselves. Moreover, in the last few years, people have not failed to use this freedom of expression to spread hatred and lies systematically.
>
> The government cannot, must not and will not remain idle when the well-being of the individual is threatened at its very roots. I am too proud of being a Quebecker not to express to you my resolution and that of the government I lead to surmount this most serious crisis.[1]

The basis of the Quebec government's reaction, according to Mr. Bourassa, was its conviction that Quebecers enjoyed very wide "freedom of expression and action," a freedom so generous that it permitted even the organized dissemination of "hatred and lies." There is a hint of righteous indignation in these words which implies that political dissenters have taken undue advantage of their freedom within the system. This part of Mr. Bourassa's case remained undeveloped, but it offered intriguing possibilities of elaboration.

More important, the statement implied further that some kinds of action outside the normal democratic process are illegitimate, and asserted explicitly that the kidnappings fell into

that category. "These actions" were "both fundamentally unjust and extremely dangerous." They challenged the stability of
Quebec's political institutions; they were unacceptable according to the prime minister's understanding of democracy. This
was not an exceptional statement of the case for orderly process within the rules of the democratic game, but a quite normal and familiar one in Canada. While Mr. Bourassa was specific about what was not acceptable—kidnapping—he did not
need to say in detail what was acceptable. The freedom of
action he mentioned obviously included the freedom to organ-
ize and compete for political power through the electoral and
parliamentary system.

This preliminary justification of the democratic order made
by Mr. Bourassa amounted to an appeal for popular support,
and an appeal to the kidnappers to recognize the dubiousness
of their own acts. It was a matter-of-form statement or a la-
ment rather than a guide to action; it offered no clear pre-
scription for dealing with the kidnappings. It is one thing to
say that such acts are unjust and dangerous; it is another
thing to say how the state should respond to them. But the
Quebec prime minister said more. Mr. Bourassa's insistence in
his remarks on the need to save the lives of the two hostages
suggested that the consideration of life was perhaps the fundamental one, overriding even the theoretical commitment to the
normal process of democracy. For a few days many persons
in Quebec took this to be the prime minister's meaning.

But on October 16, Mr. Bourassa adopted a different position in defence of War Measures. He claimed that because the
state's authority had been challenged, and because there was a
possibility of further challenges, the state could take no risks,
but had to act by all means to preserve itself.[2] Here his justification ceased to depend upon any theory of democracy. It
descended instead to the Hobbesian position that authority
rests ultimately on the successful use of power rather than upon
consent, and that, in the extreme, the state may use whatever
means it thinks necessary to maintain itself. This combination
of a shallow liberal commitment to the democratic process and
a deeper dependence upon justification by force was the persist-

ent theme in the case for the use of War Measures.

Prime Minister Trudeau never displayed Mr. Bourassa's hesitation in considering the use of force by the state. Three days before the adoption of War Measures, he had broadened the definition of the challenge to society, and made clear hints about the necessary response:

> You know, I think it is . . . important to get rid of those who are committing violence against the total society and those who are trying to run the government through a parallel power by establishing their authority by kidnapping and blackmail. . . .
> I think the society must take every means at its disposal to defend itself against the emergence of a parallel power which defies the elected power in this country and I think that goes to any distance.[3]

The references to a "parallel power" appeared odd at the time, because few observers had yet elevated the FLQ to that level of importance. The prime minister must have had more in mind than two kidnappings and a list of ransom demands. By expanding the limits of the threat, the prime minister was preparing the justification for an extraordinary official response. Kidnappings may be relatively small-scale, uncoordinated acts of defiance against authority by a few persons. (As in fact those of October turned out to be.) Trying "to run the government through a parallel power . . . which defies the elected power" is a challenge of an altogether different scale.

The reference is dangerously obscure. It raises the spectre of a full-scale effort to overthrow the government, although it never says this precisely. Did the prime minister have only the FLQ in mind, or was he already hinting at knowledge of another "plot" by other persons to create a "parallel power" and usurp authority in Quebec? Ron Haggart and Aubrey Golden, in their book *Rumours of War*, conclude that:

> His dark references to the "parallel power" meant not only the FLQ, but also the Ryan suggestion, taken far out

of context and given excessive significance in the tense atmosphere of Quebec and Ottawa.[4]

Perhaps the words were merely careless. It may be impossible ever to recover their precise intent, but at least they suggested that there was a basic challenge to the monopoly of political power held by the Bourassa and Trudeau governments and the state they represented. For Mr. Trudeau, that kind of challenge to established authority was illegitimate, and justified a very severe official response. The prime minister said that in theory his response to the challenge could go "to any distance." In the event, the response involved the first peacetime use of war emergency powers. What the prime minister was claiming was that because his government held power legitimately, it could act in any way it wished in dealing with the crisis. *In any way it wished.*

At the point of violent challenge to the established order, Mr. Trudeau was inclined to respond with an equally intransigent exertion of will and authority. The prime minister's intellectual commitment to measure and balance seemed to be suspended; now the "law of necessity" rather than the law of reason would dictate events. In November, 1970, at the National Liberal party policy convention, speaking of the "liberal ideal," the prime minister justified the use of War Measures in the language of will and self-preservation:

> Life is confrontation, and vigilance, and a fierce struggle against any threat of intrusion or death. We are unworthy of our ideal if we are not ready to defend, as we would life itself, the only roads to change that respect the human person. We are equally unworthy if we are not able to harden ourselves temporarily, but for as long as may be necessary—however repugnant it may be to do so—in order to safeguard and strengthen our democratic institutions and our highly evolved society.[5]

But the possibility of reconciling liberty and democracy, on the one hand, with confrontation and fierce struggle on the other

hand, is not nearly so easy or automatic as the prime minister
implies. The dilemma remains unresolved in Mr. Trudeau's
theory of politics.

Political authority, for the prime minister, is granted essentially through the electoral system.[6] Those who had organized a
"parallel power" had directly defied the legitimate elected representatives of the people. Whether he was speaking of isolated
FLQ cells or an organized provisional government, in either
case the principle of their challenge to authority was unacceptable to the prime minister because they had no popular mandate. There was no way they could obtain that mandate except
by entering the electoral competition and coming to power
through victory at the polls. For his government, there could
be only one acceptable means of challenging its authority: at
the next election, in the polling booth. On the other hand, any
possible acts the government might undertake were either justified in advance by the party's victory in the general election of
1968, or could be justified in retrospect by a fresh victory at the
next general election. In this plebiscitary view, the only responsibility which can be imposed on democratic governments
is the responsibility to leave office after an electoral defeat. Mr.
Trudeau made his theoretical position clear in his television
address to the nation on War Measures.

> And if any doubt exists about the good faith or the ability
> of any government, there are opposition parties ready and
> willing to be given an opportunity to govern. In short
> there is available everywhere in Canada an effective mech-
> anism to change governments by peaceful means. It has
> been employed by disenchanted voters again and again.[7]

Because there exist in Canada effective electoral mechanisms,
it is not acceptable to challenge governments except peacefully
through the electoral process.

Mr. Trudeau, like Mr. Bourassa, had proposed a fair weather theory of democracy inadequate to the occasion. The fact
was that an element of the public had rejected the democratic
process and resorted to coercion to achieve its objectives.

Faced with that challenge, the federal prime minister also became a Hobbesian absolutist rather than a democrat. The normal rules were suspended; force would now meet force, and the
stronger would win. Fair weather commitment to electoral democracy, and foul weather commitment to force, were the two
elements of the official position, riding roughshod in tandem
through a more complicated traditional theory of democracy in
Canada. The democratic problem is how to replace government
by coercion with government by consent; and neither an over-
emphasis upon elections as the source of legitimacy nor an
emphasis on the role of force can be reassuring to those who
believe in the theory of democratic consent. Paradoxically, the
two apparently contradictory theories of legitimacy easily com-
plement one another in practice.

What was worrying about Prime Minister Trudeau's reaction
was the apparent ease with which he contemplated the suspension of basic liberties and their judicial guarantees. Democracy
is exceedingly fragile if the liberties on which it depends can be
suspended whenever a small group of determined men choose
to harass it. The comprehension of democracy which permits
such easy resort to emergency measures is not supple enough to
sustain democracy in a period of prolonged internal crisis.

But that comprehension is not something new or unreflected
in Mr. Trudeau's thought. The notable feature of his discussion
of democracy in *Approaches to Politics* (written in 1958) is its
confusion about the nature of authority. While apparently
making the case for certain inalienable human rights and for
popular consent as the source of legitimate authority, Mr. Trudeau stumbles over what he sees as the state's necessary and
primary monopoly of the means of violence. In fact, electoral
democracy seems to come off second best in the Trudeau theory, as a handmaiden to and civilizing influence upon a state
that exists at bottom by exercise of force. Rather than arguing
that popular sovereignty is a means of protecting the public
against forceful coercian *by the state* (as the liberal democrat
must), he argues from the Hobbesian position that the state's
monopoly of force is necessary to protect citizens *from each
other.* A democratic system then means that the majority uses

the state's pre-existing authority for its particular purposes. Mr. Trudeau offers no fundamental protection, in theory, against the misuse of the state's power, especially if it is used by agents who command a popular majority. In his eyes, that simply makes the state more invulnerable to challenge. His electoral-authoritarian dualism is already evident in *Approaches to Politics*. But this earthy realist defence of democracy is offset at times in *Approaches* by a highly romantic, utopian vision:

> democracy appears as the logical outcome of a policy aimed at preventing tyranny, avoiding violence, doing justice to all, encouraging the full flowering of personality, and turning to account the creative liberty of every citizen.[8]

Once Mr. Trudeau descends from the heights of rhetoric to a realistic explanation of democracy, he adopts a static and fragile theory: that electoral majorities create legitimacy, and that they always rest upon the prior establishment of the state's monopoly of force.

The theoretical commitment to balloting as the key democratic instrument had the most immediate practical consequences. The kidnapping crisis occurred in the middle of a Montreal civic election campaign. The sudden arrival of the Canadian army in Montreal, the unexpected imposition of War Measures, the unusual efforts of Jean Marchand and Jean Drapeau to link the local opposition party (the Front d'action politique) with the FLQ, and the arrest of two of its leading candidates for civic office (they were later released without charge), led some prominent persons to doubt whether the vote (scheduled for October 25) could take place in a sufficiently fair atmosphere of public calm.[9] They requested the Bourassa government to postpone the date of the election until the crisis had passed, as the provincial government had the power to do. The events, in their view, had seriously intimidated the political opposition to Mayor Drapeau's Civic Party, and made it impossible to seek a normal public judgment of the candidates for office. The case for delay was, by any reasonable standard of fair play, a strong one. Quebec City, however, refused to inter-

vene; the election took place, and Mayor Drapeau and his
party swept the slate clean.[10] The mayor pronounced this a
triumph for democracy. For him, and by default for the Bourassa and Trudeau governments who chose not to intervene,
only the statistical result of the ballot appeared to matter. The
conditions and atmosphere in which the balloting took place
were of no account.

A theory of democracy which focusses so narrowly upon the
act of casting a ballot, and not at all upon the circumstances in
which this may occur, can accommodate many more serious
political abuses—although those preceding October 25 were
serious enough. Mayor Drapeau obviously shares Prime Minister Trudeau's commitment to electoral democracy. But the
theory, interpreted so narrowly, is a pathetic and dangerous
caricature of democracy in the Canadian tradition.

According to this reductionist theory of democratic legitimacy, there can be no doubt that an attempt to influence government policy by kidnapping, or an attempt to broaden or replace a Quebec cabinet propelled into office only six months
earlier by an election victory, are illegitimate acts which must
be resisted in order to defend the system. The theory justifies
the defence; but the theory is a highly oversimplified abstraction which is inadequate as an account of the normal work-
ings of Canadian democracy. To insist upon applying it strictly in practice would disrupt and soon destroy the democratic
system, and result in its replacement by a system of plebiscitary dictatorship.

The legitimacy of authority is not established in Canada simply by the casting of ballots on election day; it is established in
a number of more complicated ways, and it can be removed,
too, by other than electoral means. Canada does not possess a
straightforward system of popular sovereignty. The relationship of legitimacy to the results of public balloting is at best
indirect.

Political leaders and their parties in Canada have increasingly campaigned as though they were acting in a system of popular sovereignty, but nevertheless there remain substantial bar-
riers, both political and legal, to its consummation. In the first

place, there is no means of expressing a direct choice for one potential prime minister over another; the popular choice is reflected in the election of 265 ordinary members of parliament. The single-member system and the multiparty system combine to assure that many MPs will be elected without majority support. The key to what party holds power is thus not the popular vote, but the number of seats held in the House of Commons. In the situation in which no party wins a majority of seats, the party holding power (quite legitimately) may command neither a popular nor a parliamentary majority. (This was the case in Canada from June, 1962 until April, 1968.) The party in power may indeed not even be the largest party in the House, if it is able to arrange (quite legitimately) the necessary third party assistance. The party in power, or the prime minister, may be legitimately changed within the term of a single parliament, without reference to the electorate. Defined strictly, the Canadian system is one of parliamentary sovereignty rather than popular or electoral sovereignty, and it is to the support of the House rather than the public that the prime minister should cater from day to day.

Legally, the situation is even more complex, for we retain the formal constitutional trappings of the monarchy with its prerogative powers, which arise not from the people but from the inherited and undefined authority of the crown. Thus, only the governor-general can legally invest the authority of office in a potential prime minister. He does not take office simply by winning a majority of seats in the House or by declaring that he has done so. The monarch or the governor-general once exercised real discretion in choosing the prime minister, and it is just conceivable, still, that circumstances might occasionally allow him to do so again—as long as the present parliamentary system remains.

One of the possibilities that the editors of *Le Devoir* considered on October 11 was that the Bourassa government might feel itself unable to carry on in the face of further terror, in which case it would have been necessary for the lieutenant-governor to call upon a potential prime minister who could re-establish the cabinet's authority. The editors believed that this might best be René Lévesque (even though he did not hold a seat in the National Assembly), and they assumed also that other prominent leaders from outside the National Assembly would have to be invited to join such a government of national unity. In the parliamentary system, this kind of extraordinary action in a crisis would be entirely legitimate, even though it would violate a narrower theory of electoral democracy.

Perhaps the alarming interpretation which was put upon the tentative Ryan proposals by Ottawa indicates a fairly wide acceptance of the electoral theory among members of the federal cabinet and their advisers. Even the description given to the proposal—of a 'provisional government'—is misleading, since it is a continental European term implying the suspension of the regular constitution. Under the parliamentary constitution, the concept is unnecessary, since the constitution permits this degree of flexibility within the system. The normal language is to call such a government a coalition, which does not shock the sensibilities.

To make these points is to do more than quibble about language and window dressing: it is rather to emphasize that the Canadian constitution is a mixed system, which lacks any clear location of sovereignty or source of legitimacy. It is misleading in both fact and spirit to claim that popular election is the simple and straightforward source of legitimate authority in Canada. To claim this is to suggest that there really can be no difficult problems of legitimacy, that they are all resolved in the ballot box. It is to suggest, therefore, that there are *no other* possible claims to legitimacy, that the judgment of the ballot box is absolute. Only in the most limited sense is this true. Canadian parties normally do accept the conventions of popular election, and accept that, every four or five years, they will fall back upon the public judgment. But that judgment, as we have seen, only works in the most imperfect and roundabout ways.

And theoretically it offers no blank cheques. In the extreme, the House, and perhaps the governor-general, may properly intervene to restrain or remove a prime minister and cabinet who blatantly abuse their authority. (Only the ingrained tradition of excessive party loyalty to the leader hides this possibility in the contemporary House of Commons.) On rare occasions, the public readily accepts the legitimacy of parliamentary obstruction *by a minority* against unduly arbitrary acts proposed by the ministry. (This remains one of the most practical and effective illustrations that the legitimacy of a government's acts is not automatically guaranteed by the election results.)

More broadly, the public's role does not cease after election day. It may quite properly, according to the popular understanding of the system, use a variety of pressures to influence governments to act in what it (or part of it) conceives to be 'the public interest.' The whole lobbying process is an expression of this continuing and proper public interest in the acts of government. Most governments readily accept the legitimacy of the process, and frequently allow themselves to be influenced by it. They do not let themselves get hung up on nice definitions of whether their authority has been challenged by such activity; they take it for granted as normal. The difficult point comes in deciding what public or parliamentary challenges really are unacceptable violations of the rules; for any system has its norms, and these can be violated.

The electoral theory of democratic legitimacy misleadingly defines away the real problem; for what it ultimately implies is that no attempt to influence government, in Parliament or outside it, is finally legitimate except the use of the ballot at election time—that is, on extremely narrow terms, on an occasion determined by the prime minister, and in conditions subject to extreme propaganda and manipulation of public feeling by those in power. Carried to its logical extreme, the theory means that any other opportunity for the expression of dissent —in Parliament, in the press or on television, through an organized lobby or demonstration, or through civil disobedience —is derivative, perhaps only allowed by the grace of those in power, on sufferance rather than in principle. At this extreme, the theory is purely Rousseauean: a virtually mystical electoral act transmits the general will to the sovereign, who alone interprets and enforces it. The expression of dissent becomes factious and potentially disloyal. The only other indications of public will which may be useful to authority—useful, though not necessary—are the results of public opinion polls. If they are favourable, they can be quoted in support of government policy, and presented as evidence of the probable *ex post facto* authorization of controversial acts at the next general election. (Lyndon Johnson the Bonapartist pondered them deeply, and departed in consideration of their omens. Pierre Trudeau and Robert Bourassa cling firmly to the memory of those figures of eighty-seven percent support in December, 1970.)

This is the logic of the pure plebiscitary theory: the country is of course not yet in the unfortunate position of living under its consistent application, although there are enough signs of a trend to cause anxiety to parliamentary democrats.

An objection might be made that this analysis is an incomplete and unbalanced account of the Trudeau government's interpretation of democracy. What about its preoccupation with "participation," which has gone farther, rhetorically at least, than that of any other national party? The answer is that no politician's collection of political attitudes is likely to be entirely self-consistent, especially during a period of crisis. The interest in "participatory democracy" reflects the prime minister's own instinct that traditional democratic institutions are in a precarious state of trial, and somehow need fundamental renewal; or it is opportunist, or both. The slogan is vaguely revolutionary, and was picked up by liberal reformers from the New Left in the mid-sixties. This is the key to its real status: for the Trudeau government, it is no more than a slogan, for its thorough application would be revolutionary and entirely unacceptable to the caucus or the party organization. At the moment of decision, when it has been forced to choose between participation and the exercise of the state's authority, the Trudeau government has always opted for authority.[11]

So far the analysis has been concerned with the procedures which establish legitimacy: in Canada there have traditionally been many, not just one. For the advocate of the electoral theory of legitimacy, democracy is only a matter of procedure. But this limitation impoverishes a potentially rich democratic theory, and weakens it fatally in the face of radical criticism. A more generous theory of democracy allows for a substantial judgment of whether authority actually performs acts which serve the interests of the citizens. An electorate sufficiently frustrated by a government which accepts the electoral rules but persistently neglects the economic, social or cultural interests of its citizens may, after a point, withdraw its obedience from that government. If an election is not imminent, or if the electoral process and the party system demonstrably offer no relief, then the question of other, less normal means of resistance inevitably arises. The current dilemma of American opponents of the Vietnam war illustrates the point. After watching the election of governments pledged to limit and end the war, one Republican and one Democratic, in 1964 and 1968, and after experiencing the deceitfulness of those pledges, what acts of resistance become justifiable?

At a distance many Canadians can accept the theoretical point that a viable theory of democracy must allow, on its fringe, for the possibility of passive or even violent resistance to authority which has lost or is losing its legitimacy. (The electoral theory allows the point too, though only in the event that the electoral process itself is suspended or seriously compromised.) Historically, the justification for democracy grows directly out of theories of tyrannicide and of popular consent as the basis of legitimacy. The point is that a sufficient democratic theory can and must accommodate the possibility of extreme challenge to authority *within the system*, and need not extrude it from understanding. There are very serious practical consequences of such extrusion, and the simple electoral theory of legitimacy, or anything close to it, can hardly avoid falling victim to these consequences in a crisis.

The electoral theory of legitimacy establishes a deceptively sharp line between what kind of opposition is acceptable in principle, and what kind is not. Opposition within the legally defined rules of the electoral process is proper; any other kind is potentially improper and at the extreme, violent intimidation like kidnapping is always unacceptable. Frequently the distinction is made between opposition that is 'peaceful,' and opposition that involves the threat or the use of force or violence; and

this distinction seems to be central to the federal case for War
Measures. But in practice it is extremely difficult to apply this
supposedly clear distinction with any precision, and the tendency then must be either not to apply it, or to extend its meaning
increasingly broadly. On the other side of the coin, the theory
does not inhibit established authority in its ability to use or
threaten the use of force or violence for *its* purposes. That is an
awkward paradox; the theory seems to reduce to the question
of whose ox is gored.

At this point the electoral theory breaks down. It offers no
guidance to those in power about how to respond to a violent
domestic challenge to their authority; and it imposes no theoretical limits upon the state's own use of force or coercion. The
absolutism of the Rousseauean legislator easily transforms itself into the absolutism of the Hobbesian sovereign. Both abso-
lutisms must be rejected by the democrat. *There are always
limits to democratic authority.* The use of violence or coercion
by the state can be as great a threat to its legitimacy as may be
their use by opponents of the regime.

The practical situation can be illustrated by three examples,
one of them hypothetical. In 1958, an attempted right-wing
military coup in France over Algerian policy threatened by
force the existence of the Fourth French Republic. The Republic could not stand in the face of the challenge, which was the
culmination of a series of attacks on its legitimacy. Under the
umbrella of this attempted coup, support mounted for the accession of General de Gaulle to power. The general sensed the
occasion, declared his willingness to accept office, and was
shortly invested with power as prime minister by the president
of the Republic. Thereafter, de Gaulle interpreted his 'mandate' in a revolutionary way, prepared a new constitution for
the Fifth Republic, had it ratified by popular vote, and himself assumed the newly powerful office of president. While
those in authority when the crisis erupted obviously considered the military challenge to be an unacceptable attempt to
establish a "parallel power," they accepted the legitimacy of
General de Gaulle's challenge; and retrospectively, so did the
electorate in its use of the ballot. De Gaulle hardly came to

power through a normal democratic process, but nevertheless the theory of democracy accepted by de Gaulle himself, by the incumbent president, and even by the French public, was flexible enough to accommodate so unusual an accession. De Gaulle had no problem of legitimacy; it was the tottering Fourth Republic, the established order, which could not defend its right to exist. In the circumstances, the public quite evidently would not have consented to a military defence of the Fourth Republic against the challenge of the general. The ghostly and ephemeral quality of democratic legitimacy was illustrated by these events: it had somehow drained away from the established institutions before the coup, and found its new location in the Fifth Republic at the inspiration of de Gaulle. Any claim for the established order based on a narrow theory of electoral legitimacy would have been inadequate and ludicrous in France in May, 1958.

Ten years later, in May, 1968, another series of events culminated in another basic challenge in France: but this time to the authority of de Gaulle and the Fifth Republic.[12] Given the complexity of the accepted theory of legitimacy, the de Gaulle government took some days to assess whether or not it still possessed legitimate authority, and in the end, early in June, the president gambled that it did and reasserted that authority successfully.[13] At the darkest point of the crisis, two established politicians made the same kind of thrust for power that de Gaulle himself had made in 1958. Pierre Mendes-France (the leader of the Radical party) declared himself ready to take office as prime minister in a new provisional government, and François Mitterand (a socialist and former opponent of de Gaulle for the presidency) announced his willingness to take the presidency. The thrust failed when President de Gaulle announced his intention of holding onto office a few days later. But the broader challenge did bring about new parliamentary elections.

In this case as in 1958, there was no serious or extensive claim that Mendes-France and Mitterand had acted unconstitutionally. Imprudently, perhaps (they failed): but they were not accused of sedition, of plotting the overthrow of the state by force; and it is almost inconceivable that charges of that sort would have been laid against them. Yet they had acted under the umbrella of, or had sought to take advantage of, a revolutionary challenge to authority which was frequently violent and out of control in the streets. Their purpose could be regarded both as personally opportunist and as patriotic: they sensed that their own accession to power might stabilize order and restore legitimacy to the system.

In the far more normal conditions of Quebec in October, 1970, there was no challenge to democratic legitimacy like those of 1958 or 1968 in France. There was no military threat; there was no threat of public disorder remotely close to what actually occurred for weeks in Paris in 1968; there was no assertion of an extra-constitutional claim to power similar to those of de Gaulle, Mendes-France and Mitterand. There was a private and tentative offer of advice from the editor of *Le Devoir* to Lucien Saulnier and Robert Bourassa, questioning whether a broadened coalition government was not desirable. Yet this advice was considered on reflection to border on sedition, and was taken into account in the decision to suspend the constitution. And there was *anticipation* of possible street demonstrations.

It seems reasonable to conclude that something more than panic or malice alone stood behind the judgment to invoke War Measures; what stood behind it was a theory of authority which could not easily accommodate the possible creation of a coalition government, nor the possibility of street demonstrations against the established public policy in the crisis. Since the theory could not accommodate these possibilities as tolerable (although extreme) elements of the system, the theory could then allow for extraordinary rather than ordinary measures to meet these possibilities. The practical dangers of an inadequate theory were vividly demonstrated by the invasion of civil liberties and the abuse of the democratic system that followed.

When legitimacy is considered to reside so emphatically and permanently in certain hands holding certain offices in a certain constitutional system, the actual ebbs and flows of authority cannot be recognized or accepted as normal events, to be responded to in normal ways. The narrow conception of legitimacy actually creates a fragile system, and encourages challenges to its fragile stability.

The analysis must go still further. While one may grant that rather special acts may become reasonable and acceptable ones in a constitutional crisis if these acts are intended to maintain liberty and the openness of the democratic order—acts like General de Gaulle's offer to take power or proposals for coalition government—and while one may grant that such acts have a higher priority than ones which limit liberty or inhibit democratic procedures, how should the state respond to undisguised *violent* threats to its integrity? Don't these challenges, at least, require an unyielding response in kind, which may offend normal democratic sensibilities? Aren't certain acts always beyond the bounds of the democratic order? The easy answer would be to say yes, a system must obviously defend itself, and there are some acts against it which can never be passively tolerated. But this answer would be wrong.

There should be no dogmatic commitment to democratic order in the abstract, no automatic commitment to use exceptional measures against certain kinds of threats to the system. This kind of absolute commitment may lead in its application to the permanent limitation of liberty and to insecurity of life, to the paradoxical situation in which a democracy destroys itself on the pretext of defending itself. This is a real and immediate possibility, not just a nice debating point.

Jacques Maritain, in his book *Man and the State*, considers the delicate matter of the limits of democratic dissent from a Catholic perspective in a section which he titles "The Prophetic Shock-Minorities."

> What I mean is that it is not enough to define a democratic society by its legal structure. Another element plays also a basic part, namely the dynamic leaven or energy which fosters political *movement*, and which cannot be inscribed in any constitution or embodied in any institution, since it is both personal and contingent in nature, and rooted in free initiative. I should like to call that ex-

istential factor a prophetic factor. Democracy cannot do
without it. The people need prophets.

And those servants or prophets of the people are not
—not necessarily—elected representatives of the people.
Their mission starts in their own hearts and consciousness. In this sense they are self-appointed prophets. They
are needed in the normal functioning of a democratic society. They are needed especially in the periods of crisis,
birth, or basic renewal of a democratic society.[14]

In a healthy democratic system, prophetic leadership may
express itself through the normal political channels. "The
happiest circumstance for the body politic," says Maritian,
"obtains when the top men in the state are at the same time
genuine prophets of the people."[15] But in periods of crisis or
"basic transformation," when new questions and new challenges are in the air, the function of those who believe they
have a special public mission becomes especially crucial and
problematic. Where in the system they may arise becomes less
predictable in crisis, although the likelihood grows that their
attitude to normal channels and established institutions will be
unorthodox, because of their very role as challengers.

The primary work of the inspired servant of the people is
to *awaken* the people, to awaken them to something better than everyone's daily business, to the sense of a supra-
individual task to be performed.[16]

Maritain affirms that this is both "a quite vital and necessary
social phenomenon" and "a quite dangerous phenomenon."

For where there is inspiration and prophecy, there are
false prophets and true prophets; thieves aiming to domi-
nate men and servants aiming to set them free; inspiration from dark instincts and inspiration from genuine
love. And nothing is more difficult than what is called
"discrimination between spirits." It is easy to mistake im-
pure inspiration for unsullied inspiration; nay more, it is

easy to slip from genuine inspiration to a corrupt one. And we know that *optimi corruptio pessima*, corruption of what is best is what is worst.[17]

Maritain names as examples of "inspired servants" the fathers of the French Revolution and the American Constitution, the leaders of the Italian Risorgimento and the liberation of Ireland, Gandhi, the early prophets of trade unionism, Charles de Gaulle in 1940. All were, in the beginning, spokesmen for minorities who claimed on faith to speak for their entire communities. All turned out in the end to be true prophets. But also, in contrast, "we have ... been able to contemplate how the makers of totalitarian States have used the power of vanguard insurgent minorities." These men, in his conception, were false prophets, deceptive guides who sought to enslave rather than free their peoples.

In the last decade of growing crisis in Canada, Maritain's historic insight into the role of prophetic missionaries offers us guidance. The crisis came first and most intensively in Quebec, and from Quebec, so far, have come the leading prophets of our possible futures. The discrimination between false and true prophets in Canada is as difficult and risky as Maritain warns that it will be. Some have risen for short periods only to disappear quickly in the turmoil; others have been more and more with us. If there are three who now stand out for our judgment, who most sharply represent the alternatives before us, and who carry our fates in their hands, they are Pierre Elliott Trudeau, René Lévesque, and Pierre Vallières: the rational federalist, the rational nationalist, and the revolutionary utopian. Each entered the realm of politics out of conviction that the established order was changing, and that the public had to be led in new paths. Each had some self-recognition of the special circumstances surrounding his entry into the public arena, and each increasingly perceives the ominous possibilities for all Canada that rest upon his individual destiny. Each offers a different formula for the country's passage through crisis to a new equilibrium. And each challenges the others and those they represent. Two of them hardly admit the presence of the third in the company of prophets. If this juxtaposition of names in similar roles offends, then consider Maritain's advice:

> The political problem we are confronted with ... is the problem of the prophetic pioneering minorities or shock-minorities—I say shock-minorities as one says shock-troops—a problem which any theory of democracy should frankly face.

It is impossible to integrate this problem into a realistic theory of Canadian democracy in 1971 without including Pierre Vallières among the prophets, true or corrupted. He and the FLQ, like the other two, pose fundamental choices to Quebec and Canada, and must occupy an equal place—without special status—in the consideration of our deepest choices.

These choices have now been thrust upon us, and cannot be ignored.

> The people are to be awakened—that means that the people are asleep. People as a rule prefer to sleep. Awakenings are always bitter.... It is a fact that, for good or evil, the great historical changes in political societies have been brought about by a few, who were convinced that they embodied the real will—to be awakened—of the people, as contrasting with the people's wish to sleep.

It is not self-evident which among these three men, and to what degree, are true or false prophets; it has not yet been decided in fact. That choice rests ultimately with the people of Quebec and Canada, and on the way to it, many things can change. The manner in which the choice is offered will have much to do with our ability to distinguish true prophets from false and to accept the appropriate leadership. The choice must be offered freely.

Maritain notes that nineteenth century thought produced "a dreadful ambiguity" about democratic theory. There was a spurious democratic philosophy, derived from Rousseau, which distrusted the people and held that they should be forced to be free. Maritain described the advocates of such practice as "betrayers of the people."

For they treated the people like sick children while they were clamoring for the rights and freedom of the people. Those who distrust the people while appealing to the highest feelings and to the blood of the people cheat and betray the people. The first axiom and precept in democracy is to trust the people. Trust the people, respect the people, trust them even and first of all while awakening them, that is, while putting yourself at the service of their human dignity.[20]

Forcing the people to be free led on the contrary to the horrors of totalitarianism, in which the people are obedient and the state is free. These horrors must at all costs be avoided in Canada. To avoid them Maritain rightly insists that democrats must clearly understand the appropriate role of prophetic shock-minorities. He summarizes that role in three points.

First, *illegal action* must always be the exception, not the rule. It can only be justified "as the lesser evil" when the minority faces some kind of illegal authority or tyrannical power.

Second, the *use of force* or harsh coercion can also only be justified in exceptional conditions, and then subject to the consideration of justice.

The use of terror striking the innocent and the guilty indiscriminately is always a crime. Innocent persons can indirectly suffer from just public measures directed to the social group in which they belong; but no innocent person should ever be punished, put into captivity, put to death.[21]

Third, while it is "the event"—success or failure—that determines whether the minority was right or wrong to claim to speak for the people, the only legitimate test of that claim is "*free approval by the people*, as soon as the people can express their will." What this means, Maritain defines in greater detail:

the use of force should always be provisional as well as exceptional, and the free consultation of the people always intended as an urgent, unpostponable aim; . . . the risk that a prophetic shock-minority is taking must be fairly taken . . . this minority would betray itself as well as the

people if it clung to power by any means whatever . . .
it must be ready to lose the game if the people say so.[22]

Obviously these strictures apply as much to prophets who
hold power in the system as they do to those who challenge it.
The public must be able to protect itself both against false
prophets and against the corruption of true prophets–those
who may set out to protect the people but who end up by
dominating them. For that purpose, Maritain insists that the
fundamental guarantee is not institutional but political and
moral:

> Nothing can replace in this connection the strength of the
> common ethos, the inner energy of democratic faith and
> civil morality in the people themselves, the enjoyment by
> them of real freedom in their everyday life and of a truly
> human standard of living, and the active participation of
> them in political life from the bottom up. If these condi-
> tions are lacking, the door is open to deception.[23]

One weapon above all that the people need to sustain this
political liberty, writes Maritain, is "the freedom of expression
and criticism . . . even at the price of great risks––still less
great than the loss of liberty."

> A free people needs a free press, I mean free from the
> State, and free also from economic bondage and the power
> of money.[24]

At this stage in the vicious game in Canada, it is necessary
for the democratic public to apply such standards of criticism
without favour to all those who claim to speak for them, and to
accept the acts and proposals of those in power no more on
faith than those of any of their challengers. And now that the
alternative options for the country have been posed to us—
whether on the hustings or out of the barrel of a gun—those
options must be considered rather than ignored. They are on
the agenda of our politics because various determined prophets
forcefully placed them there. It is futile now to suggest that the

country should not have to face unpleasant questions. The prophets have stirred us from our slumbers, and we must judge their claims. In doing so, no one of them must be permitted to frighten or intimidate the public into making its choice under duress.

The democratic system in all its disorder and confusion, in all its openness to abuse, must be sustained while Quebec and Canada, in the next few years, work out their destinies in freedom. The use of private terror in the name of a prophetic view, the limitation of civil liberty through emergency legislation, the unscrupulous manipulation or intimidation of the electorate, the use of fear or blackmail as political weapons from whatever source, all these must be condemned and rejected. Now that the Canadian system is in crisis, democrats cannot afford to lose their nerve or their understanding. The risk that Quebec and Canada may come out of the crisis with fundamentally altered constitutions, and transformed economic and social systems, must be accepted in freedom. Priority must always be given, in the transition and in the outcome, to the concrete protection of human life and human liberty. Unless these human conditions are met, authority is sure to lose its way, and what might have been best will have become worst.

6: The federalist dogma

An adequate examination of Ottawa's response to the kidnapping crisis of 1970 requires analysis from still another perspective. In that response, there were significant elements of surprise, confusion, indecision, and for a few days, some degree of panic; there was misunderstanding of the FLQ; there was the difficulty in the dominant theory of democracy of comprehending how political violence could be dealt with except by resort to extraordinary measures; and there was a further, equally fundamental political factor at work. This was the official set of attitudes and policies relating to the future of Canadian federalism, best expressed (once again) in the writings and speeches of Prime Minister Pierre Elliott Trudeau. In a manner unusual for a country not previously given to theoretical speculation about its institutions and its policies, the views of one man have come increasingly since 1966 to represent the authorized version of Canadian political thought, and to reveal most accurately the rationale behind the policy of the federal government. Perhaps this is not entirely remarkable, for the absence of theoretical political discussion in English Canada meant that when a talented theorist came along—writing with pungency in both languages—the large gap was easily filled, and many observers were awe-stricken at the result.

Mr. Trudeau's reputation as a theorist (for those who cared about such things) was already substantial when he entered federal politics in 1965. What is most notable is that, having elaborated his theories about French-speaking Canada, nationalism, federalism and individualism, he was then catapulted into the position in which he could apply those theories to practice, "a result," he pleads, "I had not really desired, or even expected."[1] In 1966, he became parliamentary secretary to Prime Minister Lester B. Pearson, in 1967 minister of justice, and in April, 1968, leader of the Liberal party and prime minister of Canada.

Mr. Trudeau's strong and articulate views on the federal constitution of Canada began to make themselves felt in the federal-provincial fiscal conference of October, 1966. By the opening of the first constitutional conference in February, 1968, they dominated the federal position, and thereafter they have been applied by Ottawa with persistent determination and to the exclusion of any other elements. Within Quebec, Mr. Trudeau has managed, first, to capture and convert the Quebec wing of the federal Liberal party from an uncertain interest in Quebec's autonomy to his own federalist views; and second, to turn the provincial Liberal party around by 180 degrees from the aggressive autonomism of Jean Lesage and Paul Gérin-Lajoie to the quietist "profitable federalism" of Prime Minister Robert Bourassa.[2]

John Saywell wrote in 1968 that "consistency is . . . the most remarkable quality of Mr. Trudeau's thoughts and actions over the past two decades."[3] Three years later, that would still be almost an accurate judgment. Feature after feature of his thought, expressed in papers written from the mid-fifties to the mid-sixties, has become incarnate in the speeches and policies of a prime minister. A vast body of followers, political and administrative, still justifiably impressed by his skills—and his authority—does not say him nay.

But as Mr. Trudeau has admitted, the practice of politics is not the practice of political philosophy. Can we be so certain that consistency is a practical as well as an intellectual virtue? Even in the realm of thought, there are limits to its utility. Complete consistency would generate an entirely closed and static theoretical system, very limited in its capacity for growth.

As we have seen, the inadequacy of Mr. Trudeau's attempt to resolve the theoretical problem of the source of political authority, coupled with the pressures of the modern party and electoral systems, have brought him to a view of electoral politics which tends in crisis to undermine the traditional strengths of the parliamentary democratic system. Now, too, in the light of the brutal acts of the FLQ, it is necessary to examine the adequacy of the prime minister's theory and practice of federalism, and the relationship of his federalist approach to these events.

Are there any weaknesses in Mr. Trudeau's thought which limit the value of its consistent application in practice? It would be the sign of an extraordinary prophet if his theoretical schemes actually fitted every occasion they were intended to; but if they do not fit, it matters a great deal to Canadians what happens next. In that case, are the theories to be altered to take account of "reality," or is "reality" (meaning the lives and fortunes of individual persons) to be adjusted to fit the theories? Mr. Trudeau holds himself to be a pragmatist in politics; but there is that nagging sense of his "consistency," which implies some commitment to absolutes. How is he consistent, and how much does it matter?

Gérard Pelletier wrote of Pierre Trudeau that he has "a genuine theory of politics—that is, a complete and coherent system of responses based on a clear conception of men and society."[4] But Mr. Trudeau himself can be our guide in assessing that kind of praise:

> I early realized that ideological systems are the true enemies of freedom. On the political front, accepted opinions are not only inhibiting to the mind, they contain the very source of error. When a political ideology is universally accepted by the élite, when the people who 'define situations' embrace and venerate it, this means that it is high time free men were fighting it. For political freedom finds its essential strength in a sense of balance and proportion. As soon as one tendency becomes too strong, it constitutes a menace.[5]

His own "coherent system" must, on his own terms, be the subject of severe critical analysis, especially since it has been carried to power in Ottawa. In the French-speaking community, an extensive analysis of the prime minister's writings has taken place over a decade; his articles were polemical contributions to a domestic debate, and they have never occupied a privileged position beyond criticism. But in English Canada, on the contrary, the weak tradition of political debate and the adulation of Pierre Trudeau the politician have tended to obscure the need for close dissection of his thought.[6]

Four closely related subjects have preoccupied Mr. Trudeau in his writings: the destructive and retrogressive nature of nationalism (including the French and English Canadian varieties); the creative possibilities of federalism (for both Canada and the world); the inevitability and desirability of technological change; and the human value of liberty. These concerns mark him as a pre-eminent advocate of modern liberal individualism; and he holds to his views on these subjects with the tenacity of the religious convert. While his massing of the arguments in defence of his positions on nationalism, federalism, technology and progress is technically impressive, it is also consistently one-sided. He grants himself all the devastating arguments; he allows no doubts; he gives his opponents the back of his hand. The result is that he comes out of his speculations with what appear to be very deep commitments, and no time for alternatives. His account of modern history is summary, closed and conventionally liberal; and from that account he can see only one acceptable pathway forward for mankind, into a future of rational, progressive, technically advanced, anti-nationalist federal societies. In his way Pierre Trudeau is as much the utopian dogmatist as Pierre Vallières. His writings take positions of virtually complete certainty about what the Canadian future should be, and what it should not be. Only the lingering strength of his commitment to liberty and democratic choice allows him to perceive the possibility that Quebec and Canada may reject the path he sees for them.

On the subject of Quebec nationalism and the independence movement, the prime minister's opinions have not changed since the early sixties. In an interview with Tom Buckley of the *New York Times* after the October crisis, Mr. Trudeau said:

> I wrote ... several years ago showing that the intelligent-sia of Quebec were detached from reality, and that the whole history of nationalism in Quebec was linked to an unreal vision of our province. I showed in those pages that, whereas history was moving in one direction, the in-tellectuals were moving in a completely different direc-tion. The result was they gave absolutely no effective leadership to the people. This can be substantiated chap-ter and verse. ... I think it is the case now. There is a failure among those Quebec leaders who are separatists to start from the facts, and the facts are the first law of poli-tics. It would be better, I sometimes say, if there were 200 million French-speaking people in North America, but there are not. ...

This was a capsule summary and reassertion of the prime min-ister's views on Quebec nationalism which had been set out at length in a series of essays published between 1956 and 1965.[8]

The "basic facts of the problem" which condition Mr. Tru-deau's response are that "no constitutional reform—indeed not even a declaration of independence—could make French a major language of business and industry in North America, or make Quebec a state capable of dictating its terms to the rest of the continent."[9] The Quebec economy is integrated "for better or worse" in a continental economy; it is dominated by "the most powerful economic giant the world has ever known. ... Capital employment and the technology tend to cross the border as a result of legislation favourable to them."[10] The French-speaking community of Canada will remain a small minority in an economically integrated English-speaking conti-nent. Mr. Trudeau does not examine with any care the range of manoeuvre that a sovereign legislature might possess in these circumstances; he takes for granted that the essential economic and demographic facts are unchanging data from which Quebec must work. The reasons why he believes this require a short excursion into his economic assumptions.

There is, in his view, a natural flow of foreign investment into stable, high consumption countries like Canada. "The result is a sort of economic dependence which is sometimes described in such emotional terms as 'colonialism' and 'colonization.' "[11] This condition of dependency should not be eliminated by "simplified solutions" like expropriation, for these could drastically affect the living standards of Canadian citizens. (No government, he suggests, should ever assume that its citizens would be willing to accept such a cut in living standards "for the mere pleasure of seeing a national middle class replacing a foreign one at the helm of various enterprises.") The acceptable option in dealing with foreign capital, he says,

> in the first place, is to use foreign capital within the framework of rational economic development; and secondly, to create indigenous capital and direct it toward the key sectors of the future: computers, services, and industry in the age of nuclear energy.[12]

Both the commitment to "rational economic development" and the "key sectors" approach are examples of Mr. Trudeau's uncritical liberal view of economic progress. Economic growth, based increasingly upon advanced science and technology, is for him an unexamined good which follows its own inevitable course:

> if laws and constitutions create a situation that is not favourable to the entry and development of technology and technicians, the country will be hopelessly outclassed economically, and its industries soon outdated and inefficient. On the other hand, if technology is free to enter, the country must irrevocably step into the era of great communities, of continental economies. It will have to pay the price in terms of its national sovereignty. And its constitutional law will have to take this factor into account.[13]

He suggests that for Quebec, state intervention to influence the future could theoretically follow either of two extremes, or a range of more moderate positions between the extremes. On one side, Quebec could achieve full independence, "thereby saving Quebec particularism by subordinating all other needs to it." The situation that would arise is radically simplified and asserted without supporting evidence:

> So much the worse if the economy is slowed down and the standard of living lowered as a result. That is the price we must pay to end the cultural alienation of a conquered and demoralized nation. When this nation has gained new confidence in itself, it will at last be able to take vigorous and economically valid action.[14]

This choice, he believes, is attractive to the economically secure middle class who will form the new ruling class of an independent Quebec.

Alternatively, Mr. Trudeau suggests that:

> We can minimize the importance of the state's sovereignty, obtain the maximum advantage from our integration into the American continent, and make Quebec an ideal province for industrial development. So much the worse if the particular qualities of Quebec (including language) must suffer: this is the price that must be paid if the people of Quebec are to attain a higher standard of living and of technical development. Their improved material position will later enable them to affirm more strongly what remains of the French fact in North America.[15]

The poorer members of the working class, as well as "those who have no reason to fear international competition—for example, true scientists or true financiers" will be inclined to favour this alternative.

> From their point of view, it is better first to free man through technical progress: to liberate him from physical misery so that he may then concern himself with culture.[16]

The context, the sponsorship of this paper,[17] and Mr. Trudeau's own appreciation of himself as a cosmopolitan intellectual, all place him unambiguously on this side of the balance. But his full position, as we shall see, is not quite at this extreme, for it offers a strategy for maintaining the French fact in North America while at the same time embracing technological progress.

The strictly economic goal of Quebec must be to enter fully into the North American economy on its dominant terms.

> In the last resort, what really matters is that the per-capita income be increased as quickly as possible. To achieve this, the economy of Quebec must become extremely efficient, technologically advanced, quite specialized, and capable of offering the best products at the best prices in all the markets of the world.
>
> In practice this means that the economy of Quebec must not be isolated, but open to the whole world, for then it will find new markets as well as the competition it has to expect.[18]

This classic statement of Manchester liberalism is accompanied by a distrust of state interference in the market economy that reflects an indifference to the problems of monopoly control, income distribution, technological unemployment, the multinational corporation, uncontrolled growth and the non-economic satisfactions of both producers and consumers. It is a statement of the economics of the bigger pie, a faith more understandable in the 1920s or the 1940s than the 1970s. And it can be applied equally to the policies of the Quebec state or the Canadian state. The liberal economist is an antinationalist; or to put it another way, he is inclined to discount the contributions to human well-being than can be made by communal and non-economic factors. There is no clear evidence to indicate that Mr. Trudeau's economic views have changed since his assumption of office.

But the prime minister's antinationalism has historic and cultural as well as economic dimensions. In three paragraphs of his essay "New Treason of the Intellectuals" he recounts a progressive history of the world, which culminates in the modern age of nationalist wars. "Some seven thousand years of history in three paragraphs is, of course, a little short," he admits,[19] but it neatly sets up his case.

> The tiny portion of history marked by the emergence of the nation-states is also the scene of the most devastating wars, the worst atrocities, and the most degrading collective hatred the world has ever seen. . . . In our day . . . we have seen nations refusing to listen to Beethoven because they are at war with Germany, others boycotting the Peking Opera because they refuse to recognize China, and still others refusing visas or passports to scholars wishing to attend some scientific or humanitarian congress in a country of differing ideology. Pasternak was not even allowed to go to Stockholm to accept his Nobel Prize. A concept of nation that pays so little honour to science and culture obviously can find no room above itself in its scale of values for truth, liberty, and life itself. It is a concept that corrupts all: in peacetime the intellectuals become propagandists for the nation and the propaganda is a lie; in war time the democracies slither toward dictatorship and the dictatorships herd us into concentration camps; and finally after the massacres of Ethiopia come those of London and Hamburg, then of Hiroshima and Nagasaki, and perhaps more and more until the final massacre. I know very well that the nation-state idea is not the sole cause of all the evils born of war; modern technology has a good deal to answer for on that score! But the important thing is that the nation-state idea has caused wars to become more and more total over the last two centuries; and that is the idea I take issue with so vehemently. Besides, each time a state has taken an exclusive and intolerant idea as its cornerstone (religion, nationhood, ideology), this idea has been the very mainspring of war.[20]

One can condemn the inhumanities that Mr. Trudeau condemns; but it is conceivable that a somewhat more complex theory of history is necessary to explain them. And can we accept the entire fairness or accuracy of a case that burdens today's Quebec nationalism with all the (purported) sins of

European nationalism? The Trudeau view at least leaves that impression.

When it descends to the level of more local explanation, the Trudeau thesis accounts for traditional Quebec nationalism as a defensive response to the expansionist nationalism of England during and after the Conquest, and to English-Canadian nationalism after 1867.[21] His critical account of Quebec's inward-turned, authoritarian and paternalist, anti-modern "state-of-siege" nationalism is the conventional one accepted by liberals and radicals of the 1950s. It ceases to be conventional, however, when he projects most of the features of this historic nationalist faith into the present and the future, and attributes them to the contemporary advocates of independence for Quebec.

> We have expended a great deal of time and energy proclaiming the rights due our nationality, invoking our divine mission, trumpeting our virtues, bewailing our misfortunes, denouncing our enemies, and avowing our independence; and for all that not one of our workmen is more skilled, nor a civil servant the more efficient, a financier the richer, a doctor the more advanced, a bishop the more learned, nor a single solitary politician the less ignorant. ... The Separatists of 1962 that I have met are, in general, genuinely earnest and nice people; but the few times I have had the opportunity of talking with them at any length, I have almost always been astounded by the totalitarian outlook of some, the anti-Semitism of others, and the complete ignorance of basic economics of them all.
>
> This is what I call *la nouvelle trahison des clercs*: this self-deluding passion of a large segment of our thinking population for throwing themselves headlong—intellectually and spiritually—into purely escapist pursuits.[22]

The prime minister's dogged consistency is evident. In 1962, he refers to his own words of 1958 about the misguided nationalists of French Canada who try "to swim upstream against the course of progress," and who thus leave the people "without any effective intellectual direction."[23] In 1970 he refers again to those same words, as though eight years of intervening history have offered no reason for the slightest reconsideration. ("I think it is the case now.")

Just as traditional Quebec nationalists have been uniformly reactionary and anti-democratic, so, for the prime minister, would be the new nationalists if they ever take power. The leftists among them would be overwhelmed by the majority of right-wing nationalists.[24] But beyond this, even the leftists would be forced by their primary devotion to the idea of the nation into reaction:

> a nationalist government is by nature intolerant, discriminatory, and, when all is said and done, totalitarian.[25]

That deceptive phrase, "when all is said and done," contains within it an astonishing dismissal of the good faith, determination and potential power of Quebec's *democratic* separatists.

A familiar feature of Mr. Trudeau's polemical method—or perhaps more, of his characteristic cast of mind—is obvious in his analysis of Quebec nationalism and separatism. This is his persistent tendency to identify his opponents as extremists and absolutists: they are never granted the respect of being reasonable, moderate, informed, or practical men. They must always be pushed to the extreme so that their claims are made to appear absurd, ignorant, irrational, frenzied, or mad. The separatist movement is the perpetuation of all that is worst in Quebec's past; it is regarded essentially as monolithic, and the strictures cast upon it are delivered without qualification:

> The fact is that at bottom the separatists despair of ever being able to convince the public of the rightness of their ideas. That long work of education and persuasion among the masses undertaken by the unions for many decades, done by the Social Crediters themselves for thirty years—for this the separatists have neither the courage, nor the means, nor, especially, that respect for the other man's freedom which is essential in undertaking it and leading it to success.
>
> So they want to abolish freedom and impose a dicta-

torship of their minority. They are in sole possession of the truth, so others need only get into line. And when things don't go fast enough they take to illegality and violence.[26]

And again:

The truth is that the separatist counter-revolution is the work of a powerless *petit-bourgeois* minority afraid of being left behind by the twentieth-century revolution. Rather than carving themselves out a place in it by ability, they want to make the whole tribe return to the wigwams by declaring its independence.[27]

The intellectual leaders of Quebec are condemned for their confusion and their failure to offer leadership. The contemporary youth of Quebec are dismissed for their failure to follow "the road to power for all who had mastered the sciences and the techniques of the day: automation, cybernetics, nuclear-science, economic planning, and what-not else."[28] They needed only "boldness, intelligence, and work" to seize the modern world, but they rejected the challenge.

Alas, freedom proved to be too heady a drink to pour for the French-Canadian youth of 1960. Almost at the first sip it went at top speed in search of some more soothing milk, some new dogmatism. It reproached my generation with not having offered it any 'doctrine'—we who had spent the best part of our youth demolishing servile doctrinairism—and it took refuge in the bosom of its mother, the Holy Nation.[29]

The whole Quebec nation, finally, is denied maturity, intelligence and dignity. If Quebecers eventually choose an independent destiny,

the ultimate tragedy would be in not realizing that French Canada is too culturally anaemic, too economically destitute, too intellectually retarded, too spiritually paralysed, to be able to survive more than a couple of decades of stagnation, emptying herself of all her vitality into nothing but a cesspit, the mirror of her nationalistic vanity and 'dignity.'[34]

Such condescension, such contempt, such disregard for degree and measure—such intolerance, must be charged with the very absolutism Mr. Trudeau attributes to his antagonists. This is the language of psychological violence, not of rational politics. It cannot be surprising that it has stimulated some responses in kind.

The prime minister's rejection of nationalism appears to be absolute; and it applies with equal strength to English-Canadian nationalism. His reading of Canadian history is that "the rational compromise" of 1867, which offered an opportunity for French Canada to develop itself in parallel with English Canada, was neglected by both sides. Canada came to be regarded as the nation-state of English-speaking Canadians. French-speaking Canadians were effectively shut out of equal participation in the national government, and driven back to their protected reserve in the province of Quebec. The idea of the nation-state led British Canadians naturally to identify "the Canadian state with themselves to the greatest degree possible."

> Since the French Canadians had the bad grace to decline assimilation, such an identification was beyond being completely realizable. So the Anglo-Canadians built themselves an illusion of it by fencing off the French Canadians in their Quebec ghetto and then nibbling at its constitutional powers and carrying them off bit by bit to Ottawa. Outside Quebec they fought, with staggering ferocity, against anything that might intrude upon that illusion: the use of French on stamps, money, cheques, in the civil service, the railroads, and the whole works.[31]

This meant that

> the French-Canadian denizens of a Quebec ghetto, stripped of power by centralization, were expected to recognize themselves in a national image which had hardly

any French traits, and were asked to have the utmost confidence in a central state where French Canada's influence
was mainly measured by its not inconsiderable nuisance
value.[32]

Canadian nationalism, then, could not provide the basis for
any lasting consensus between the two language groups.

   To this point, Mr. Trudeau's account of the French-Canadian experience in confederation is one that he shares with
Quebec nationalists. Seen from the present historical perspective, it is also an interpretation of Canada's first century that is
broadly accepted by many English Canadians. (Although it is
typically oversimplified, and attributes too much conscious,
conspiratorial purpose to English-Canadian leaders. A great
deal can be explained less dramatically simply by the innocent
cultural parochialism of English-Canadian politicians, and by
their preoccupation with national economic development after
1867.) But in his response to this history, Mr. Trudeau de-
parts from the nationalists. He rejects their "defensive" response, and argues instead that English-Canadian nationalism
must be challenged and transcended. This is possible, he believes, because in reality it has always been feeble; it has dominated Canada because French Canadians have passively allowed it to do so. It has "never had much of an edge"; it has
"never enjoyed a crushing predominance and has never been
in a position to refuse all compromise with the country's prin-
cipal national minority...."[33]

   If Canada as a state has had so little room for French
   Canadians it is above all because we have failed to make
   ourselves indispensable to its future ... with the sole exception of Laurier, I fail to see a single French Canadian
   in more than three-quarters of a century whose presence in
   the federal cabinet might be considered indispensable to
   the history of Canada as written—except at election time,
   of course, when the tribe always invokes the aid of its
   witch-doctors. Similarly, in the ranks of senior civil servants, there is probably no one who could be said to have
   decisively and beneficially influenced the development of

our administration as has, for example, an O.D. Skelton,
a Graham Towers, or a Norman Robertson.

Consequently, an examination of the few nationalist
'victories' carried off at Ottawa after years of wrangling in
high places will reveal probably none that could not have
been won in the course of a single cabinet meeting by a
French Canadian of the calibre of C. D. Howe. All our
cabinet ministers put together would scarcely match the
weight of a bilingual cheque or the name of a hotel.[34]

French Canadians can take the heights by direct, individual
assault. In doing so, Pierre Trudeau believes, they have a per-
fectly adequate instrument in their hands, the B.N.A. Act and
its division of powers—providing they use it with force and
skill. But what they must make of Canada is a community
beyond all nationalisms, "a truly pluralistic and polyethnic society."[35]

When he comes to this positive side of his vision, Mr. Trudeau takes wing again, as in his economics, into romance and
abstraction. The man who accepts his challenge will be universal man, "the fully-developed man of intellect" who has somehow risen above the restricting identity of his national past.

Where civilization has pushed ahead in spite of all, it is
where the intellectuals have found the strength within
themselves to put their faith in mankind before any national prejudice. . . . 'Man,' said Renan, 'is bound neither
to his language nor his race; he is bound only to himself
because he is a free agent, or in other words a moral
being.'[36]

So Quebecers and Canadians cannot expect any emotional
sops in the future as seen by Pierre Elliott Trudeau; they must
defeat sentimentality, and become men of pure and abstract
intelligence. That is the only way to unify Canada; the emotional alternative is unacceptable:

Even if massive investments in flags, dignity, protection-
ism, and Canadian content of television managed to hold

the country together a few more years, separatism would
remain a recurrent phenomenon, and very soon again
new generations of Canadians and Quebeckers would be
expected to pour their intellectual energies down the
drain of emotionalism.[37]

Instead, reason and social science offer us escape into the para-
dise of technology.

> In the world of tomorrow . . . the state—if it is not to be
> outdistanced by its rivals—will need political instruments
> which are sharper, stronger, and more finely controlled
> than any based on mere emotionalism—such tools will be
> made up of advanced technology and scientific investiga-
> tion, as applied to the fields of law, economics, social
> psychology, international affairs, and other areas of hu-
> man relations. . . .[38]

The proper vehicle for such rarefied intelligence, according
to Mr. Trudeau, already exists *in potentia* in Canada—the federal state. It is the pre-eminent "product of reason in politics,"
because it is the result of a compromise or a pact which aimed
at overcoming cultural particularisms. And the Canadian example offers itself to the world as a guide:

> It would seem, in fact, a matter of considerable urgency
> for world peace and the success of the new states that the
> form of good government known as democratic federalism
> should be perfected and promoted, in the hope of solving
> to some extent the world-wide problems of ethnic plural-
> ism.[39]

Just as Quebec nationalism must carry the burdens of modern
history's disasters on its shoulders, a renewed and refined Canadian federalism must carry the equal burdens of all righteousness, reason and hope. For us, mere mortals, the citizens
of Quebec and Canada, these burdens may be too heavy to
bear. Must the political system really be loaded with the
weights that Pierre Trudeau thrusts upon it?

The kind of federalism promoted by the prime minister is

purified and balanced, a system in which functions and resources would be allocated rationally to the levels of government most suited to perform particular tasks. The encroachments of the central authority upon the jurisdiction of the
provinces that grew in the centralizing era of 1930 to 1960
would be systematically removed. If Ottawa or the provinces
genuinely desired to transfer authority up or down, this would
henceforth be accomplished openly through constitutional
amendment or an agreed system of delegation. There would be
no provision for any basic differentiation in status among the
provinces, for 'special status' would lead—in the prime minister's logical universe—to an inevitable slide toward independence. The existing patterns of empirical compromise between
Ottawa and the provinces that neglect or short-circuit the provisions of the B.N.A. Act would be replaced by orderly
schemes of liaison and cooperation. The result would not be
the centralized and disorderly federation that English Canadians have grown accustomed to since the Second World War,
but "the freedom and diversity arising from federative decen-
tralization."[40] The Trudeau constitutional system possesses the
appeals of reason and order, but it lacks place for the empirical
accretions of history and constitutional diplomacy, additions
that exist, however illogically, because they have permitted the
constitution to work (more or less) in the face of unexpected
pressures and historical changes.

The two prime examples of the prime minister's application
of reason to the Canadian constitutional situation are his proposal for an entrenched bill of rights, and his recommendations
for the extension of bilingualism in federal services across the
country. These are his fundamental suggestions for constitutional change, advocated quite specifically in his writings before he entered politics, and the chief objects of his concern in
formal constitutional discussions since 1968.[41]

The prime minister's bilingual and bicultural policies (to extend guarantees for French-language minorities on the model
of existing guarantees to the English-language minority in
Quebec, and to equalize the opportunities for advancement in
the federal service for both language groups) are so close to the

language recommendations of the Royal Commission on Bilingualism and Biculturalism that Mr. Trudeau's persuasive influence upon the Commission is evident. As in his conception of federalism, so in his view of bilingualism, Mr. Trudeau is a firm legalist and utopian.

> At the federal level, the two languages must have absolute equality. With regard to legislative and judicial functions, this is already theoretically the case, according to Section 133 of the constitution; but the theory must be completely incorporated into actual practice so that, for example, any law or ruling is invalid if the English and French texts are not published side by side. Like the United States, we must move beyond 'separate but equal' to 'complete integration.'
>
> With regard to the executive functions, innovation is clearly required. Of course, it would be difficult to test the bilingualism of ministers of the Crown, and no doubt the whole thing will rest upon which men the voters decide to elect. (But it might also be decided by the fact that unilingual ministers would become frustrated when decisions were sometimes taken in French, and sometimes in English within the cabinet.) Everywhere else, and notably in the civil service and the armed forces, the two languages must be on the basis of absolute equality. This concept of equality must also be put into effect by management and by the courts ... if a knowledge of English is required in the higher echelons of the civil service, then the same should be true of French. It is obvious that if such rules were applied overnight, they would result in a great many injustices and might indeed bring the state machinery grinding to a halt. But the introduction of such reforms must nevertheless be carried out according to a fixed schedule set by law. . . .[42]

If the successful achievement of these goals is to be the real test of Confederation's value, then it is safe to say now that Confederation has failed. Since 1960, the English-Canadian provinces have shown a generous and persistent spirit of toleration toward the French-language community that is unprecedented in their history. The attitude of cultural imperialism that Pierre Trudeau condemns in English Canada's past has very largely disappeared; the community seems mature and self-confident enough not to require that crutch any longer. A series of changes in the law and in administrative and educational practice across the country, extending opportunities for the use of the French language, have been made in growing knowledge of the country's previous neglect for its French-language minorities. The transformation of the cabinet into a bilingual institution has been accomplished by the most competent team of French-speaking ministers since 1867. These are all notable achievements of determination and goodwill.

But the prime minister demands too much; the record of anxiety in the federal civil service over discrimination in hiring, and the uneasiness expressed in Parliament in 1969 (especially by prairie members) over the Official Languages Act, are only two indications of the practical limits of bilingual policy outside Quebec, Ontario and New Brunswick. The English-Canadian approach to such matters is empirical and practical, the result of a sense of fairness rather than of the acceptance of a formal principle. The very French inclination to push the matter to its fundaments of principle and to enshrine the principle in law strikes English Canadians as doctrinaire and extreme—particularly if the law is bound to be a dead letter in some parts of the country. More than that, it can easily be interpreted as a means of intimidation, or a paternal guide laid down from on high to subjects who cannot be trusted to act with justice on their own. ("Such reforms must certainly be incorporated into constitutional law. It would not be very realistic to rely upon good will or purely political action.")[43]

English Canada, in spite of its goodwill, is unlikely to go along with the prime minister in his attempt to establish a complete system of working legal guarantees for bilingualism. The real practical progress that has been made need not and should not be abandoned, but the limits of the experiment are closer than the prime minister has yet conceded.

What is more, the exercise is basically misguided if it is regarded as the *central* means of protecting the French-speaking community from assimilation. Outside Quebec, where French Canadians are the cultural minority, there is strong evidence that the rate of assimilation to the English-speaking community is increasing, and that the provision of advanced educational opportunities in French actually speeds, rather than slows, assimilation.[44] Inside Quebec, the whole effort to extend the use of the French language in the rest of Canada has been regarded by nationalists as at best a secondary concern, at worst an irrelevancy and a diversion, from the moment that the Royal Commission on Bilingualism and Biculturalism was created in 1963. The massive federal effort has done nothing to weaken the growing popular strength of the independence movement in Quebec; if anything it has added to its strength because nationalists have considered it to offer them a false alternative. The criticism is not that the Bi and Bi effort has been in vain, but that it has been expected to do things it could never really do. This means that it has involved an abstract exercise about justice and human rights, too divorced from the realities of historical circumstance and political power to touch the problem of Quebec's relationship to Canada. If the Commission was not in origin a product of Mr. Trudeau's reason, in result it became so.

The effort to entrench a bill of rights in the constitution reflects the same exaggerated reliance upon legal abstractions at the expense of political judgment. It should have been obvious to the prime minister that the provinces would reject the proposal that they surrender their control over "property and civil rights" to the Supreme Court of Canada. Mr. Trudeau's judgment of the need for a bill of rights arose out of his experience of Quebec's frequent contempt for basic rights before 1960.[45] While generally rejecting paternalism, he relents on this matter as he does on the official languages: basic rights should be put out of reach of the legislatures because politicians cannot be trusted to protect them. But Prime Minister Diefenbaker recognized in 1960 that it would be futile to ask the provinces to abandon responsibility over civil rights, and proceeded instead to have Parliament enact a Bill of Rights covering exclusively federal matters of jurisdiction.

If there has been any change in provincial opinion on the matter since 1960, it has been in Quebec. There, two governments increasingly jealous of their rights, and wishing to expand Quebec's constitutional authority, held power from 1960 to 1970. They too rejected many features of Quebec's past; they regarded themselves as newly competent spokesmen for French Canada; they were not likely to begin constitutional discussion by agreeing to diminish Quebec's legislative powers. And yet Mr. Trudeau went into the first constitutional conference of February, 1968, arguing that a breakthrough on a constitutional bill of rights would be the first great step to a renewed Canadian federation.

> I venture to say that, if we are able to reach agreement on this vital aspect of the over-all problem, we will have found a solution to a basic issue facing Canada today....
> I believe that, once we have agreed on a Bill of Rights, an amending formula, and a system of final adjudication, little would stand in the way of a general constitutional conference to discuss such other particular changes as may be necessary to adapt our constitution to the requirements of our day.[46]

Of course the breakthrough did not occur, and three years later the constitutional conference still muddles along in its fruitless pursuit of agreement on the issue. The primacy given to the question was misguided; the subject has been a source of frustration and diversion to the conferences, which has prevented concentration upon the central question of Quebec's powers under the constitution. While Quebec nationalists may be forgiven for regarding the bill of rights as a typical device of Mr. Trudeau for avoiding their real claims, it may also be more generously regarded as another product of his abstract intellect, judged important in principle for its own sake and unaffected by recent political experience.

In 1967, when the federal government reluctantly agreed to enter into constitutional discussions under pressure from Quebec and Ontario, Quebec's objective was to convince the other provinces of her need for expanded legislative authority, and to seek their agreement in a new constitutional settlement which would grant that authority. Ottawa recognized the strength of the pressure from Quebec, but was determined from the beginning to avoid discussion on Quebec's terms. The strategy was Pierre Trudeau's, and it arose from his antagonism to the nationalist movement in Quebec in all its variations and degrees. Quebec could not be granted a status different in principle from that of any other province; what the constitutional conferences had to do, instead, to satisfy Mr. Trudeau was to achieve the legal protections for the French language and fundamental rights that were basic to his orderly constitutional model.

For Quebec, Ottawa's approach to constitutional discussion has thus offered three years of growing frustration. The Johnson, Bertrand and Bourassa governments have each asserted Quebec's demands for enlarged jurisdiction in the fields of social, cultural and economic policy; and in response, Ottawa has raised a smokescreen, introducing proposal after proposal which avoid the issue of Quebec's legislative powers. In the hope of altering the pressure at the source, federal ministers supported and assisted the accession of Robert Bourassa to the Quebec Liberal leadership in early 1970, because Mr. Bourassa promised to concentrate upon Quebec's economic development rather than upon its constitutional claims. The Bourassa victory in the election of April, 1970, was greeted with relief and satisfaction in Ottawa, because it seemed to confirm the practicality of Ottawa's approach. But even Mr. Bourassa could not free himself from the constitutional pressures that had built up over a decade, and at the February, 1971, conference he, like his predecessors, had to make the case for Quebec's expanded constitutional authority (particularly in the field of social policy). Ottawa still showed slight inclination to concede, and Mr. Bourassa returned to a Quebec National Assembly which reflected Quebec's endemic sense of frustration over the constitutional impasse. The impasse cannot be broken unless the federal government abandons its monolithic opposition to Quebec's constitutional demands, and that monolithic opposition remains, essentially, because of the prime minister's vision of

Canadian society and the strength of his will.

For the governments of the other provinces, most of them not deeply informed about the Quebec political situation and indifferent to the theoretical schemes of the prime minister, the constitutional conferences have become a bore, a puzzle, and an annoying distraction from what they regard as more essential matters. The process has been for them, in a sense, a cheat. They came to Ottawa in 1968 under the impression that there was an urgent constitutional crisis; the Royal Commission on Bilingualism and Biculturalism had written in 1965 that "Canada, without being fully conscious of the fact, is passing through the greatest crisis in its history,"[47] and many politicians and observers had echoed the concern in the succeeding three years. The Confederation for Tomorrow Conference of the provinces sponsored by Ontario in November, 1967, crystallized the national sense of urgency about fundamental constitutional reform.[48] What seemed to matter by 1968 was some kind of substantial new settlement with Quebec over its role in Confederation. But the federal government systematically diverted the constitutional conferences from meeting this challenge. The confusion and impatience of the English-speaking provinces over what has proven to be a fruitless and irrelevant process is entirely understandable. It has not been their ignorance, indifference or intolerance that has brought the conferences to failure; rather, it has been Ottawa's calculated disregard for the essentials of the political crisis.

The one set of events which has given a renewed sense of urgency to the constitutional discussions has been the October crisis. Following the crisis, the federal government came to believe that tangible progress had to occur in the talks, in order to demonstrate that accommodation was possible between Quebec and the rest of the country, and that revolutionary acts were unnecessary to achieve that accommodation. A round of intensive bargaining was therefore undertaken by Ottawa, aimed at producing agreement on patriation of the constitution from the United Kingdom, an amending formula, and some limited alterations and additions to the constitution. Two constitutional conferences, in February and June, 1971, were devoted to discussion of a "package" of constitutional reforms of this nature. But the package failed to meet the minimum claims for enlarged jurisdiction of the Bourassa government (let alone of its more nationalist opponents). Whatever sympathy the constitutional charter of June, 1971, may receive from the governments and legislatures of English Canada, therefore, it is unlikely to appease the legislative ambitions of Quebec. It remains based upon the assumption that Quebec must not be treated differently under the constitution than any other province; and so it fails to satisfy either the symbolic or the practical constitutional needs of that community.

The sad failure of the constitutional review has been reflected also in the anticlimactic demise of the Royal Commission on Bilingualism and Biculturalism. Under the guidance of the late André Laurendeau, the Commission intended to interpret its mandate widely because it understood the dimensions of the crisis. The introduction to the first volume of the final report, published in the autumn of 1967, stated the Commission's intention to publish a last volume in which the Commission would finally "approach important constitutional questions concerning the relations and the future of the two societies."[49] But this last volume never appeared. In March, 1971, the co-chairmen of the Commission wrote to Prime Minister Trudeau requesting the official dissolution of the Commission on March 31, 1971, without submission of its proposed reports on the mass media, arts and letters, the Supreme Court, Parliament, and broader constitutional questions. The commissioners explained that constitutional discussions had proceeded so far that the Commission's original intention to examine these questions had been overtaken by events, and that, in consequence, the members could not agree either on what constitutional questions they should consider or what opinions they should express if they were to consider them.[50]

The prime minister replied that "I understand completely the motives that have led you to take this decision," and accepted the termination of the Commission's work without criticism. He noted that:

It is evident that the existence of this Commission and

the nature of its reports and recommendations have already had an immense influence in the country. . . . The work of the Commission will have a beneficial, profound and durable effect upon our national unity and the progress of a country where two language groups must live together.[51]

Conveniently, the published reports of the Commission had treated the language question in a manner consistent with the approach of the prime minister. But entry by the Commission into straightforward discussion of the central constitutional questions would have raised issues at the formal level which the Trudeau government prefers not to see raised. The decision of the Commission to dissolve rather than enter the area of controversy coincided with the strategy of the federal government, and was another sign of the straitjacket into which the debate has been forced by Ottawa. Claude Ryan described the Commission's demise as "the betrayed dream of André Laurendeau," and lamented that

> if ten open-minded men, for the most part indifferent to local or partisan political considerations, cannot reach agreement [on the fundamentals of the problem], how can one hope that politicians will come to any other conclusion than a similar deadlock, or at best, to horse-trading which will also fail to bring us to a solution?[52]

The Commission failed in the end because it was constrained by the federalism of Pierre Trudeau. Its failure was a warning of the prospects for further constitutional discussion on the prime minister's dogmatic terms.

This depressing record of political failure, which has been concealed by the apparently contradictory electoral victories of the federal Liberals in 1968 and the Quebec Liberals in 1970, has another significant dimension. One of the chief means of entry for French Canadians into the uplands of creative federalism, as perceived by Pierre Elliott Trudeau, has been the political means. True to his own challenge, Mr. Trudeau and his Quebec colleagues took the heights of the Liber-

al party, and transformed the federal cabinet into a bilingual
institution. There are now some French-speaking C. D.
Howes, and that is a credit to Quebec and to Mr. Trudeau's
opportunism. But as he notes, in federal politics Quebecers
have chosen to concentrate their influence in the Liberal party, and the Liberals have prevented "the growth in Quebec of
a federal nationalist party."[53]

> They learned to cater to French Canada's intuition that
> its destinies would be better protected at Ottawa by a
> more or less independent bloc within the party in power
> than by a nationalist party, bound, because of its ethnic
> base, to remain forever seated on Opposition benches.[54]

Mr. Trudeau, too, has catered to that intuition, and has actively sought to polarize opinion in Quebec between the federal
Liberal position and the nationalist one. In doing so, he has
undermined what little opportunity might have existed for any
significant, alternative French-speaking representation in Ottawa. As long as the nationalists choose not to contest federal
elections, the field is left by default to Trudeau federalists or
Caouette federalists; and a competent Quebec politician who
seeks influence in Ottawa has no choice but to enter the Liberal
party.

Thus, as long as the political and constitutional options for
Quebec remain radically simplified between Trudeau federalism
and independence, the permanence of a leading French-speaking role in the federal cabinet—something obviously desired by
Mr. Trudeau—depends upon the maintenance of the Liberal
party in power. While that "trade-off"—a guaranteed role of
prominence for French Canadians in federal affairs at the cost
of continued Liberal power—may be acceptable to Quebec federalists, it is unlikely always to be acceptable to English Canada. In the immediate future, the consequence of English Canada's defeat of a Liberal government will probably be, among
other things, to transform the cabinet once again into an English-speaking institution. Even that notable example of bilingualism in Canada rests, in the current situation, on the most
fragile foundation. If the federal Liberals do succeed in the

short run in suppressing nationalist pressures from Quebec, in
the longer run the reappearance of an English-Canadian government in Ottawa is bound to exacerbate these pressures. This
is so, paradoxically, partly because the prime minister chose to
perpetuate Quebec's attachment to the Liberal party when he
entered politics in 1965. The dilemma is not one that can be
easily escaped; what it illustrates is the complexity of the relationship, and the depth of the influences which lead to conflict
under the present political and constitutional arrangements.

Prime Minister Trudeau has, indeed, been consistent in his
attitudes to Quebec and Canadian federalism: relentlessly consistent to the point of fanaticism. He has seen Quebec caught
in a constricting historical vice, captured and held down in the
grip of its fearful, reactionary nationalist leaders. And he has
seen the way of release. For the whole of French-Canadian
society he demands the same escape from its sterile past that
he himself has chosen—into self-disciplined, cosmopolitan, liberal individualism which transcends the ties of nation. The
convert projects his own personal liberation onto an entire society, and then, as politician, seeks to force the evolution.
George Grant has remarked on this quality of the prime minister's beliefs:

> In Mr. Trudeau's writings there is evident distaste for what
> was by tradition his own, and what is put up along with
> that distaste are universalist goods which will be capable
> of dissolving that tradition. Indeed this quality of being a
> convert to modern liberalism is one cause of his formida-
> bility. Most English-speaking liberals have lived in uni-
> versalism much longer. They have not come to it out of
> something different, but have grown up in it as their tra-
> dition. They are apt, therefore, either to accept it auto-
> matically or even to start to be cynical about its ability to
> solve human problems. On the other hand, Mr. Tru-
> deau's espousal has behind it the force of his distaste for
> its opposite against which he is reacting. Recent converts
> are especially effective exponents of a system because they
> have the confidence of believing they are doing right.[55]

The application of so strong a will, in so rarefied a cause,
to the course of Quebec's and Canada's history, has encouraged in Quebec the growth of an entire spectrum of theoretical and practical opposition to Trudeau federalism. The range
of choices before Quebec was always limited; but Pierre Trudeau, by his rationalism, has radically narrowed and distorted
those choices. And the major dialectical opponent that his approach has created is not René Lévesque the pragmatist, but
Pierre Vallières the fellow absolutist. The triangle of forces in
which Pierre Trudeau is caught as both agent and victim—and
Canada along with him—has taken the shape of classical tragedy.

7: Quebec's choices – and Canada's

The prime minister long ago took up political battle against the separatist movement in Quebec. It was his anti-separatism that brought him into federal politics in 1965; it was his opposition to special status for Quebec that dominated his concerns when he took the party leadership and campaigned for victory in the general election of 1968. In contrast to the appeasing sentiments of the Pearson government, and to the similar (but more vague) inclinations of the Conservative and NDP opposition in 1968, Pierre Elliott Trudeau alone, of the major party leaders, offered an articulate and unyielding policy on the future of Quebec. Whatever the reasons for his election victory, it was interpreted as a mandate for the prime minister's Quebec policy, and that policy was pursued systematically at succeeding dominion-provincial conferences and in the federal government's dealings with the province. Outside Quebec, the Trudeau victory of 1968 was misguidedly interpreted as a triumph for Canadian nationalism, and it effectively halted the fuzzy and inconclusive public debate on Quebec's future. The predominantly English-speaking Conservative and New Democratic parties were thrown into confusion by the result, and thereafter virtually abdicated thought on Quebec until the October events.

Inside Quebec, the 1968 election marked a corresponding clarification and hardening of attitudes for and against Trudeau federalism. The byzantine diplomatic manoeuvring which had seemed appropriate to the Lesage and Johnson governments in their dealing with the federal administrations of John Diefenbaker and Lester Pearson now proved fruitless against a prime minister of such clear intention and firm will as Pierre Elliott Trudeau. Ottawa demonstrated its resolution against Daniel Johnson and Jean-Jacques Bertrand; in response the Union Nationale government of Quebec displayed its irresolution, and was driven nearer to division between its separatist and federalist elements. Meanwhile, in a perhaps natural course of evolution—but one that was assisted by the catalytic effect of Pierre Trudeau's federal victory—separatist forces came together outside the traditional party structure under the leadership of the renegade Liberal, René Lévesque, first in his Sovereignty-Association Movement, and then, in 1968, in the moderate socialist Parti Québecois.

Even earlier, the sudden awakening of Quebec to the modern world after 1960, with its accompanying disorder and explosive vision of new possibilities, had spawned the sporadic violence of the FLQ. In the mid-sixties revolutionary separatism acquired its theoretician, just as federalism acquired its own literary advocate. Pierre Vallières passed through a period of tutelage and encouragement under Gérard Pelletier and Pierre Trudeau at *La Presse* and *Cité Libre*, gradually working out his general critique of society as Trudeau and Pelletier hardened their federalist and anti-nationalist attitudes. For the FLQ, Pierre Vallières provided the analysis and the rationale for terrorism; for Ottawa, Pierre Trudeau provided the analysis and the rationale for inflexible anti-separatism. By 1970, a series of historical accidents brought this sectarian conflict of intellectual extremes to the level of public struggle affecting the whole country.

There is no doubt that the tenacity of each man's commitment to his own ideal owes something to his explicit rejection of the other's. Pierre Vallières was one of the most prominent separatists known to Pierre Trudeau when he wrote his general condemnation of separatist narrowness and dogmatism. And Pierre Trudeau was a particular target of scorn for Pierre Val-

lières, as Trudeau progressively revealed his federalism to the
young radical writer.

> Who could have sworn, in 1963, that in Ottawa, Trudeau
> would become the number one enemy of French Canadi-
> ans, that Pelletier would agree to occupy a stall in the
> federal stable he had so often indignantly denounced, that
> Marchand would forsake the union movement to ally him-
> self with the official spokesmen of American imperialism:
> men like Pearson, Martin, Winters, Sharp, Hellyer . . . ?[1]

In 1963 Pelletier and Trudeau appointed Pierre Vallières editor of *Cité Libre*, only to discover that his radicalism was too
hot to handle.

> From the very first issue . . . we became suspect in the eyes
> of Trudeau and Pelletier. Then we denounced cooperative
> federalism, gave our support to the Parti Socialiste du
> Québec, and began to define a policy which on all points
> was at variance with the "politique fonctionelle" of Tru-
> deau. . . . Finally, we went so far as to attack directly the
> former co-editors of *Cité Libre* in an article entitled "The
> Bumblers in Power" (March, 1964), which was followed
> by a number of provocative pieces, such as "Charity, a
> Capitalist Hoax" by Jean-Claude Paquet and "Defense of
> the Iroquois" by Gérald Godin. This last was a defense of
> the "wicked, atheistic separatist" and a satire on the
> "good Huron," that is, the resigned, Christian, groveling
> federalist. That was enough to make Pelletier and Trudeau
> decide to put an end to the "experiment."[2]

Vallières was forced to resign from the editorship. His bitterness and personal animus spill over on the next page of his
book.

> Trudeau and Pelletier could not believe that the young
> people whom they had influenced from 1950 to 1960 had
> become separatist. It was as if they had given birth to a
> monster. And the young people, for their part, could not
> get over the fact that their former idols had aged so rapid-

ly. . . . Today in Ottawa, Pelletier and Trudeau cannot understand that they are traitors or that they are serving the imperialist aims of the United States and English Canada. But they are too intelligent to be considered irresponsible. That is why it is impossible not to regard them as traitors.[3]

Their own strength of will, and the forces behind them, carried the two antagonists progressively to the point where the attitudes they sponsored jointly shook the stability of the democratic process in Quebec and Canada. It would be easy to make too much of the personal relationship between Vallières and Trudeau, and to suggest that Pierre Trudeau is responsible in some self-conscious way for the most fanatic elements of opposition to his federalist policy. But it would be equally mistaken to ignore the relationship of opposites, and to suggest that the escalation of terror had nothing whatever to do with the hardening of Ottawa's attitudes against the more moderate advocates of Quebec's independence. When moderate hopes are undermined, some impatient and frustrated men move to the extremes, and extremists are tempted to act. Pierre Trudeau's policy has been to undermine the moderate separatists, to welcome and invite "confrontation" on the issue of federalism versus independence for Quebec, to speak quite carelessly as though there is no real distinction between democratic separatists and extreme terrorists. It was shortsighted, to say the least, not to foresee the ominous consequences of this approach. But English Canada allowed itself to be taken in by the reassuring blandishments of Trudeau federalism, and failed to reckon the costs.

The particular fanaticism of the FLQ cannot be understood unless one sees it within this broader framework of attitudes and responses. Pierre Trudeau himself has hinted at this understanding of the events in which he is locked; but Gérard Pelletier shows little comprehension of the tragic play of forces in his account of the October crisis, and it is little appreciated outside Quebec. Yet if Canada is to escape from an increasingly brutal confrontation in Quebec which elevates violence and repression to normal features of our political life, and which correspondingly limits the possibilities of free public choice, we must condemn and reject the polarization of forces between the two inflexible extremes.

One could take the fatalist position that it is "the situation" which narrows our choices to those at the two extremes; and this was, in a sense, the apology of Ottawa for its severe response in October, 1970. Democracy was forced to defend itself. But democracy is not served by fatalism; it cannot survive such abdication. The blackest future for liberty and free choice in Quebec—and by extension in the rest of Canada—lies in the prospect of renewed violent acts by the FLQ and repressive counter-measures by the governments. There is very little doubt that in such a contest the power of the state would be superior to that of the terrorists. But if used repeatedly as it was in 1970, that exercise of the state's power would intimidate the general population, dissipate the democratic opposition, and mock the claim that Quebec will be able to choose its future in an atmosphere of freedom. Repeated or permanent use of emergency powers would not suppress terrorism, because the movement would be permanently transfused with disenchanted recruits from the failing democratic middle. If the terrorists have chosen permanent terror, and the two governments cannot escape their predisposition to respond with extra-constitutional measures, then the province of Quebec will soon enter the condition of the Hobbesian state of nature, where men live in perpetual fear of violent death, and the life of freedom is "solitary, poor, nasty, brutish and short."

This reading of events presupposes a certain view of the public will, and of the condition of legitimacy of the federal constitution in Quebec. When Gérard Pelletier condemns what he regards as complacency toward the FLQ among democratic separatists in Quebec,[4] he is unwittingly making the same point. There is one sense in which all separatists are closer to one another than they are to the federalists (notwithstanding the abyss which lies between the social democracy of the Parti Québecois and the revolutionary zeal of the FLQ). The conflict between federalists and separatists is not political competition in the normal sense of the phrase, in which the parties broadly share objectives and methods but differ on marginal details. Rather, the conflict is over the legitimacy of the state as it is presently constituted. All self-conscious democratic separatists, like the revolutionary separatists, have already made a fundamental shift of loyalties. While the democratic separatists accept that the battle should be carried on according to the accepted rules of the game, they have made a potential commitment to withdraw their allegiance from Canada and the province of Quebec, and to transfer it to an independent Quebec under a new constitution. In April, 1970, twenty-four percent of Quebec voters, or more than thirty percent of French-speaking voters, supported candidates for the Parti Québecois;[5] in February, 1971, in the Chambly by-election, thirty-two percent voted Parti Québecois.[6] This demonstration of public support for an independence party, especially when it is interpreted against the election results of 1966 and the trends of support for the other parties, indicates that the federal state had been drained substantially of its legitimacy in Quebec before the events of October, 1970.[7]

None of the facile attempts to put a reassuring face on the Bourassa victory as a decisive reassertion of Canadian unity —and there were many, by Quebec Liberals, Ottawa correspondents and English-language editorial writers[8]—can disguise this erosion of legitimacy. Robert Bourassa came to power with what appeared in conventional terms to be a strong mandate: a large plurality of the vote and an overwhelming majority of seats in the National Assembly. But this would have been an accurate interpretation of the situation only if there had been no significant support for the independence party. The result demonstrated, instead, that consent for the Canadian union had been withdrawn by almost one quarter of Quebec voters. Any government taking office with that handicap was bound to be enfeebled.

There was perhaps the possibility that the separatist vote was a flash-in-the-pan, and that a self-confident and shrewd Quebec government might succeed over four years in drawing back substantial numbers of PQ voters to the federalist position. Both federal and provincial Liberals seemed to believe this to be a real prospect in 1970, providing that the ills of the Quebec economy could be treated adequately. But this assumption was faulty on two grounds: first, because the economic malaise was more complicated than Keynesian liberals had understood, and less amenable to their remedies than they hoped; and second, because the alienation from federalism was essentially social and political rather than economic in its origins, and never was open to exclusively economic remedies. A loss of legitimacy is not so easily reversed as a decline in employment.

There is evidence enough in the evolution of the independence movement over ten years to indicate that it is not a flash-in-the-pan, that the draining away of commitment to the Canadian state is chronic, strongly motivated, and irreversible by democratic means. The Trudeau government's strategy since 1968 has been to meet the challenge head on, in the expectation that open political confrontation would finally force the majority of Quebecers to make the sensible choice for Canada and against romantic illusion. This democratic strategy was not working decisively, however; and in October, 1970, it was abandoned temporarily for more questionable means of persuasion in the face of terror. If Ottawa returns permanently, as it should, to the normal methods of democratic persuasion, the progressive loss of the federal state's lifeblood of consent in Quebec will continue. Faced with that prospect, the response of reasonable men should not be to despair or panic, but to make the best of the opportunities that are created. Tragically, that may be asking too much of politicians whose political imagination is crippled by a nineteenth-century conception of political union and the purposes of the state.

Given the force and momentum of the separatist movement, Ottawa had a number of options open to it in 1968. It chose, and the country accepted, the Trudeau option of unyielding confrontation with Quebec nationalism. It might have made other choices. It could have continued to pursue the Pearson government's policy of *ad hoc* concessions to Quebec nationalism, granted under pressure. Or it could have taken the opportunity created after the Confederation for Tomorrow Conference to enter confidently into negotiations on the redistribution of legislative powers, in an effort to meet quickly the basic demands of Quebec for expanded legislative authority. Feeding the ambitions of Quebec in either of these ways would not have smothered separatism any more than denying those ambitions has done. But it might, for a time, have dampened down the terrorist extreme and kept open an entire range of more moderate constitutional alternatives. That policy would not have been permanently acceptable to English Canada, however, and at some point the simple question would have arisen, as it has arisen now: is it permissible for Quebec to secede peacefully from Canada? For liberal democrats, as opposed to liberal defenders of vested interests or vested power, the answer can only be yes.

Canadians outside Quebec must recognize that what is at stake is not the political existence of Canada: only abject defeatists and crypto-Americans need argue that Quebec's independence will be followed by the political disintegration of the rest of the country. The paradox of that argument is that it is the present government of anti-nationalists in Ottawa—dedicated to a dessicated unity—which is indifferent to the continuing and vigorous assertion of the Canadian national spirit. Just as he rejects Quebec nationalism, so the prime minister extends his logic to a parallel rejection of pan-Canadian nationalism. And the claim that the country cannot survive Quebec's separation can be turned back on its pessimistic advocates: the suppression by force of the independence movement in Quebec would do more to break Canada's spirit than would the peaceful promotion and achievement of Quebec's independence.

What is at stake for French-speaking Quebecers is the life or death of a national community. Now that Quebec has decisively rejected its parochial past and chosen to enter the modern world, the assimilative pressures of an English-speaking continent at last threaten to engulf it.[9] Quebecers' desire to protect their language and collective existence, which until recently took the form of defensive retreat into social and political reaction in the land and in the church, has now been transmuted into a confident and open determination to make their own destiny as free men. This is not an ignoble ambition. If any community can be said to deserve the opportunity for political independence, Quebec today is that community. Like Poland and Ireland, it has lived through generations of political and economic subordination without losing the sense of itself and its latent desire for independence as a community. What right has Canada, the legatee of a colonial conquest, to deny Quebec's independence if it makes that choice in freedom? What national virtue could the forceful denial of independence possibly strengthen?

But the fearful warnings of Pierre Trudeau ring in our ears. Do we wish to see Quebec economically impoverished and burdened with a harsh right-wing dictatorship? This is a dark vision out of Quebec's past, not an accurate prophecy in 1971 — unless the democratic institutions of contemporary Quebec are ruthlessly manipulated even before independence. They have been growing stronger for ten years. Pierre Trudeau's devastating assessment of the shortcomings of democracy in Quebec applied to the dark ages before 1960.[10] It was an assessment that was accepted and taken to heart with complete conviction by many modern Quebec nationalists. In organization and style as in the commitment of its leaders, the Parti Québecois is the most democratic party that Quebec has known in its history; and thousands of Quebecers have gained an active experience of liberty and democratic institutions for the first time in the last ten years. Of course that experience may have been heady and shallow; of course it does not guarantee political stability and liberty after independence. Men and institutions are always frail in crisis. But neither, as the growing tensions and disruptions of the decade have shown, does federalism automatically guarantee security of life and property, or political freedom, or the occasions for calm and rational political choice. Each of the prospective alternatives open to Quebec today involves great political risks. None offers ease and automatic security, except for those persons who live in illusion. Prime Minister Trudeau's astringent federalism will not transport Canada to the purified uplands of Actonian reason where passion is unknown, because that very federalism is born of passion like any other political creed, and lives on the public emotions that it has called forth. If federalists do not recognize this, they are the self-deceiving victims of pride.

Who, among the prophets, speaks most convincingly for the genuine aspirations of the Quebec public? Pierre Vallières and the FLQ raise recurring questions about capitalism and centralised power which demand more profound attention in the era of overkill, genocide and technology-gone-wild than they did when first posed in the nineteenth century. But their answers to those questions are no more satisfactory than the anarchist answers of 1870. They offer romantic sustenance to the revolutionary spirit in the course of struggle, but no realistic guidance in how to administer the community humanely after the revolution. The familiar expectation of a new human consciousness born of revolution is a will-of-the-wisp.[11] The accompanying commitment to the full use of modern technology leaves the utopia of the FLQ with the same intractable problems of defining the public interest, and asserting it through political action, as liberal democracies face so uncertainly today. In the end Pierre Vallières is as complacent and myopic about the benevolence of technical progress as Pierre Trudeau: because they are both, finally (as are we all), children of the liberal dream.

And Vallières is false to his own democratic intent. He foresees a free movement of the great majority leading to the emancipation of Quebec; but he encourages the intimidating use of violence by a revolutionary élite which destroys the possibility of free popular choice. He is, as Pierre Trudeau correctly judged, the revolutionary who cannot trust the public choice nor wait in patience while it is made. He is not the prophet of democracy and humanity for Quebec.

Nor for the present is Pierre Trudeau. His commitment to an abstract model of federalism, in defiance of the realities of Quebec opinions and sentiments, has brought to the surface the inherent contradiction between his belief in liberty, on the one hand, and his belief in order, authority and anti-nationalism on the other hand. The resolution of this contradiction has not yet occurred, and until it does his relationship to the democratic tradition in Quebec remains uncertain. He has publicly declared since October, 1970, that if the majority in Quebec were to choose independence it would be improper to prevent its achievement by the use of force.[12] But he has also used the state's power in a more immediate situation in a manner that could only shock and disrupt the rational democratic process. That experience may bring some significant modification in the prime minister's attitude to the use of power in future; or his party, recognizing the dangers better than he does, may restrain him on another occasion; or the electorate may sense the dangers and refuse to renew his mandate. But these are all slight prospects.

The prime minister is a man of will; the Liberal party is not known for its spirit of insubordination; and the electorate trusts authority in a crisis. Given those forces, the prospects for civil liberty and the peaceful evolution of politics in Quebec are not good. As George Grant warns:

> In English-speaking Canada it seems that Mr. Trudeau's status will remain high. He has come through on his promise to deal strongly with separatism. That he deals with it quite outside the principles of constitutional liberties does not seem important, because although these traditions of law were the best part of the British tradition, they are not something that can hold masses of voters' minds in the age of technological rationality. Civil liberties can be a supplementary issue in times of bad employment or in connection with other failures of the system, but they cannot be a determining issue for many voters who live within modernity.[13]

The country probably faces more severe tests of its failing democratic resilience before the matter of the prime minister's basic commitment is resolved. We are at the mercy of his will. Outside the Waffle group in the NDP, the opposition parties offer English Canada no intelligible alternative to the prime minister's inflexibility on Quebec.

The most straightforward test of Mr. Trudeau's basic commitment—and ours—would be a Parti Québecois victory in a general election in Quebec, but before that occasion arrives, there remains the likelihood of further acts of provocation by the FLQ. In such morally murky situations, before the next Quebec election, the die is likely to be cast. The indiscriminate use of emergency powers to check the "erosion of public will" a second or third time would effectively shatter democracy in Quebec for as long as the federal union remains. That option is now hardly open for a federal government which comprehends the meaning of its own democratic faith; but the October events revealed that the democratic faith is confused and feeble in Ottawa.

Does this mean that the governments of Canada and Quebec must be left disarmed before the defiance of a terrorist attack, or a genuine revolutionary uprising? The answer is no, but the question is complex. The governments have a responsibility to maintain the democratic constitution, and this means above all to maintain the atmosphere of security in which opinion on public questions can be freely formed, without intimidation from any source. Terrorists and revolutionaries can demonstrably create terror; and authority must respond in a way which both restricts specific acts of terror and calms the public mood. The state has an arsenal of regular means to do these things: it can use all the appropriate instruments of normal police activity; it can provide special protection for persons and property that may be in danger; it can reinforce the police, if necessary, with auxiliaries from the armed forces; it can use the Criminal Code to prosecute those suspected of overt criminal acts; it can reassure the public with the confident *voice* of authority. In an unexpected situation it must do such things quickly in order to prevent an epidemic of public fear.

Authority must aim its response at containment of the terrorists and reassurance of the general population, and it must do this with extreme precision. What it cannot do is to use the authority of the state to shock or intimidate public opinion. It cannot, that is, legitimately use techniques of scare, or arbitrary police action, or emergency measures to meet an "erosion of

public will," because the "erosion of public will" is a euphe-
mism for the free evolution of public debate.

In October, 1970, the use of emergency measures was condemned out of the mouths of federal ministers themselves.
While the police and Prime Minister Bourassa speculated des-
perately about the imminence of selective assassinations and
the revolutionary seizure of power, the minister of justice, John
Turner, made no such claim. He ingenuously defended War
Measures on the ground that there had been this dangerous
"erosion of public will." Allaying public panic was one thing—
it was a proper objective and it could have been done without
invoking War Measures. But the public whose will was "eroding" was not in a state of insecurity or panic. The erosion was
occurring among opponents of the Liberal governments who
favoured a different response to terrorism. They were emotionally affected by the acts of terror; but they were deliber-
ately exercising their freedom as citizens to advocate one particular kind of reaction. The use of emergency powers to suppress that political option was a partisan act directed against
democratic opponents and the general opinion which they
sought to influence. It was an act of intimidation rather than
a responsible act of democratic authority.

It is extraordinary, in retrospect, that the federal cabinet
would admit to the use of War Measures for this purpose; for
the ambiguity of the situation permitted that motive to be dis-
guised or denied. If the intent had been denied, the result
would nevertheless have been the same, and equally unacceptable. For the shock effect of proclaiming emergency powers (in
combination with the consequent murder of Pierre Laporte)
destroyed for the time being the conditions under which a genuine public assessment of the situation could be made. Under
those two hammer-blows, public judgment was disrupted. Two
faits accomplis brought a landslide of support to established
authority; but it was not, in spite of the reassurance Pierre
Trudeau drew from it, the kind of support which sustains a
democracy.

We have consistently underestimated the importance—the

nearly decisive weight—of the accomplished fact in recent events. The accomplished fact deadens the spirit of public action, which is at the heart of political freedom, and it teaches people not to think or feel.[14]

The *New Yorker* recently made this comment about the U.S. administration's exercise of power in relation to the Vietnam war; and it applies equally to the Canadian use of War Measures.

Public judgment exercised *after* the imposition of emergency measures cannot be considered a fair measure of unfettered popular opinion. The eighty-seven percent support for the use of War Measures was, in fact, monolithic evidence that the public trust had been abused. The governments did not permit opinion in Montreal to move to its own conclusions about how the terror should be relieved: instead, when those in power read signs indicating that opinion was moving noticeably against their policy of ambiguity and delay (but only then), they acted to shatter that trend of opinion. This was the offence to democracy. There are, certainly, some means of "defending democracy" which are profoundly subversive of it. This kind of manipulation of opinion can easily become a habit, and the public can lose its ability to recognize the insult it has received. It is simpler to render the electorate punch-drunk than to sharpen its critical sense.

There may be, it is true, terrorist or revolutionary situations so serious that the society enters a condition of civil war. In those circumstances, the discussion of liberty and democracy becomes at least temporarily academic, and more elemental considerations of preserving life take precedence. But it is a grotesque error of judgment to consider that Canada has reached that situation. The error of judgment was committed by those who invoked War Measures, and it is not an error that a democratic electorate should tolerate.

Democracy does not possess the full means of responding to terrorism that an authoritarian regime does. It must depend, in the end, on the completely free expression of public choice, in the hope that the public will repudiate terror. If that choice is suppressed or distorted by the terrorists or the authorities, the very foundation of the system is undermined. *Democracy has no legitimate defence against the erosion of public will except the normal means of democratic persuasion.* It has defences against violent terror or armed revolution, but it must act with such discretion in applying them that it does not confuse that defence with the imposition of undue pressure on the public will.

In the event of renewed terrorism, the alternative should thus be to contemplate what was unthinkable for the governments in October, 1970: to meet the challenge by rejecting extraordinary measures and concentrating instead on creating a Quebec government of national unity commanding the support of all sections of the population except the most intransigent terrorists and federalists.[15] This government could negotiate terms with the terrorists without fearing for the loss of its own authority in the process. Its demonstrated confidence and authority might drive the terrorists into a relatively long period of inactivity.

Such a government would have to include René Lévesque, some other respresentatives of the Parti Québecois, and some National Union members. Its formation would mark a dramatic change of direction for the Quebec Liberal party, for the provincial party would have to move somewhat closer to the independentist position of the Parti Québecois in order to gain its adherence. A coalition of this kind would be directed, in fact, against both federalist Ottawa and against terrorism. The project is not one that the Trudeau government would appreciate, without a revolution in its own predispositions. But short of a deliberate and calm reversal of policy on federalism in the Quebec Liberal party before the next provincial election (which remains possible), this sort of realignment in crisis offers the best hope for the Quebec Liberal government to meet another terrorist challenge, and to recover its independence from Ottawa and its integrity before the Quebec electorate. The coalition would probably not survive into an election campaign, but the terms of that competition would be radically altered, and the Quebec Liberal party would have prepared the ground for its continued existence as a major party after Quebec achieves its independence. For the sake of democracy after independence, this preparation is vital. The hindrance is that Robert Bourassa has not yet demonstrated the strength of character or breadth of imagination which would lead him to take such a bold initiative in defiance of federalist orthodoxy and the federalist forces which brought him to power.

Preferably, the Front de Libération du Québec will measure its folly of October carefully and refrain from serious acts of terror before the next Quebec election. In this event Ottawa and Quebec City will have no trace of justification, even on their own terms, for the renewed use of emergency powers. The political atmosphere of Quebec will return to relative calm, and the restored momentum of the Parti Québecois will lead it closer to a majority in 1973 or 1974. In these conditions the eventual victory of the Parti Québecois, which now forms the only coherent and substantial opposition to the party in power in Québec, is almost assured.

The probabilities under ideal democratic conditions are the ones which democrats must be prepared to accept. The actual conditions will be less than ideal, but frank acknowledgment in advance of the legitimacy of a Parti Québecois victory, if it should occur, would do something to diminish the existing stresses on the democratic system in Quebec and assist its survival. One of the sanctions for terrorism in Quebec is the uncertainty over whether independence is possible through peaceful evolution: we must grant that possibility as one means of disarming terror. Canada must utterly reject the choice of putting down the Quebec independence movement by the threat or use of armed force: this rejection is what the admission of Quebec's right of self-determination means.

In English Canada, such an explicit acknowledgment by the leaders of all federal parties would purge the atmosphere of a potentially poisonous spirit of intolerance, and permit us to use our energy, instead, in conceiving workable new constitutional arrangements with Quebec in friendship. As much as the confusion of events allows us to perceive, René Lévesque and the Parti Québecois come nearer than any other politicians in

Quebec today to fulfilling the role of true prophets. They most of all appear determined to respect the public and to risk its decisions in freedom. The rest of Canada should not fear that admission.

A philosophic release from the constrictions of Pierre Trudeau's federalism would only bring Canada to the beginning of an intricate negotiation. If that negotiation can be undertaken in confidence and trust on both sides, there are still few reasons why the outcome should not benefit the spirit of both nations, and leave us freer than we are in 1971 to pursue our modest national goals. But if confidence and trust have disappeared, our hearts will bleed in vain. And so will Canada.

Notes

CHAPTER ONE

1. Prime Minister P. E. Trudeau, quoted in Toronto *Daily Star*, October 10, 1970.

2. House of Commons *Debates*, October 5, 1970, p. 8709.

3. House of Commons *Debates*, October 6, 1970, p. 8836.

4. Anthony Westell in the Toronto *Daily Star*, January 16, 1971.

5. René Lévesque is quoted in Ron Haggart's and Aubrey Golden's *Rumours of War* (new press, Toronto, 1971) as saying of a conversation with Robert Bourassa on October 14: "About the kidnappers, Bourassa said: 'Those kids, after all, those kids are from our own neck of the woods and basically they aren't bad, they won't kill.'" (p. 28). In his book *La Crise d'Octobre* (Editions du jour, Montreal, 1971), Gérard Pelletier says that he always had the intuitive feeling that the cell holding Mr. Cross would not carry out their threat to kill him (p. 105).

6. Pierre Nadeau of the CBC recorded a filmed interview with two FLQ activists in the Jordan desert during the summer of 1970 in which they spoke of proposed "selective assassinations." See also the article by Ron Lebel, "The Fixed Terror of Quebec," *The Globe Magazine*, September 19, 1970.

7. In the fourth and fifth communiqués from the Liberation cell (*Le*

Devoir, 8 octobre, 9 octobre, 1970). Claude Ryan, in an editorial in *Le Devoir* on October 9, noted that the fifth communiqué confirmed the previous impression that "the seven initial demands do not form an indissoluble whole."

8. In his *Le Devoir* editorial on October 9, Claude Ryan mentioned such considerations but rejected them as less important than the need to save Mr. Cross's life by an agreement to release prisoners.

9. Toronto *Daily Star*, January 16, 1971.

10. While the Speech noted with some anxiety the unusual pressures for rapid change imposed on the world by "the forces of science and technology," and mentioned several other subjects of national concern, it ended with this reassurance:

> Notwithstanding its difficulties, Canada continues to enjoy social stability to an exceptional degree.
>   This stability is not simply a matter of luck. Good fortune is a factor, but we should accept gracefully the fact that we are also more amenable to reason and, perhaps, more capable of wise decision than we are normally willing to admit. The burden of our European inheritance and our fascination with our American neighbour tend often to distract us and cause us to be unaware of that reasonableness and that wisdom. We forget to our own disadvantage, for these are traits that have made Canada a land of freedom. Canadians should pause on occasions such as this to reflect that their country is regarded by others with envy. It is a high place of liberty in the world. It is held in esteem because in Canada respect is paid to the individual; privacy and freedom of thought are honoured. Among us, each citizen, each community, finds its roots in liberty. Our national entity does not depend upon a melting pot, but is a concerted exercise of free will.
>   It is in this sense of liberty as a supreme value, and of tolerance as its social and political expression, that we find our foundation and strength as a people. Let us recognize with pride and with modesty what so many strangers admire and see in us: that we have achieved greatly, that in the future even greater achievements are within our reach.
> (House of Commons *Debates*, October 8, 1970, p.3.)

Ironic words.

11. But Premier Bourassa cancelled visits to Los Angeles and San

Francisco because of the kidnapping crisis. (Toronto *Daily Star*, October 9, 1970.)

12. Perhaps the 'Operations Centre' was meant to serve more than a public relations role, and was genuinely regarded by its organizers as a vital element in the federal government's response to terror. The emphasis of the Centre on communications and technique reflects a recurrent theme in the Trudeau administration's approach to the art of government, a preoccupation with the role of the electronic media in contemporary politics. This preoccupation was also reflected during the crisis in the deference paid by members of the prime minister's staff to the views of Marshall McLuhan. McLuhan was consulted, and "gave his opinion that the terrorists had made sophisticated use of the media, particularly radio, to draw public attention." (Anthony Westell, Toronto *Daily Star*, January 16, 1971.) Westell added that "experts who analyzed FLQ communiqués and statements said they made skilful use of images and symbols to exploit social discontent." This is obscurantist sleight of hand, meant to give the impression that there is a mysterious expertise about such judgments available only to initiates but not to ordinary mortals. But the judgments were surely commonplaces, and not to be exaggerated: propagandists use whatever means are available to them, and good propagandists use them well. The danger of the preoccupation with the media is that it diverts attention from more fundamental factors in the crisis (such as those suggested in chapters four, five and six) and that it leads to consideration of policies for control of the media–that is, censorship–which, if adopted, are not only inefficient but also a major new source of public grievance.

13. See, for example, the article by David Crane on the weekend consultations between Mr. Trudeau and Mr. Bourassa, in the Toronto *Globe and Mail*, October 12, 1970.

14. Toronto *Daily Star*, October 9, 1970.

15. See Anthony Westell's comment on the erosion of the government's position, Toronto *Daily Star*, October 13, 1970.

16. Toronto *Daily Star*, October 10, 1970.

17. *ibid.*

18. Toronto *Globe and Mail*, October 12, 1970. While External Affairs Minister Mitchell Sharp had spoken for the two governments

throughout the week, this final statement of position was delivered by the Quebec minister of justice. The calculation that went into that shift of focus was reported in the Toronto *Daily Star* on October 12 by John Doig:

> Why, then, was the federal government silent on Saturday afternoon, as the 6 P.M. deadline for the "execution" of Cross crept nearer?
>
> Why was a Quebec cabinet minister charged with the duty of giving Canada's answer to the diplomat's kidnappers?
>
> Sharp revealed the official reasons to the *Star* in an interview last night, and other federal government sources filled in the background details of the decision.
>
> Officials said federal and provincial government strategists bargaining to save the diplomat's life had to consider, among other things, the political climate of Quebec and the apparent attitude of the province's people to the kidnapping.
>
> They concluded that the overwhelming majority of Quebeckers were horrified.
>
> They believed, also, the sources said, that the people of Quebec at large would be sympathetic to any stated declaration that the province's government would seek to reform its institutions by democratic processes, and not under the threat of violence.
>
> But that message, because of Canada's delicate federal nature, could be delivered only by a Quebecker—and a member of the Quebec government.

19. In his speech to the twenty-fifth commemorative session of the United Nations General Assembly on October 14, 1970, the Hon. Mitchell Sharp said: "Individual nations can refrain from using force and violence in international relationships. They are not compelled to devote ability and resources to produce nuclear weapons and others equally capable of mass destruction. . . . Individually, we can act within national boundaries to ensure that the dignity of man is assured." (Toronto *Globe and Mail*, October 15, 1970.)

CHAPTER TWO

1. Toronto *Daily Star*, October 13, 1970.

2. Quoted in Toronto *Daily Star*, November 9, 1970.

3. Hon. Otto E. Lang, in a letter to the author, October 22, 1970. (Quoted by permission of Mr. Lang.)

4. October 17, 1970.

5. *The Manchester Guardian Weekly*, October 24, 1970.

6. Quoted in the Toronto *Daily Star*, October 9, 1970.

7. Toronto *Globe and Mail*, October 12, 1970. The Toronto *Daily Star*, in an editorial somewhat misleadingly headed "Our safety demands smashing the FLQ," also asked the governments "to bargain with the kidnappers–that is, to exchange FLQ men in jail for the British diplomat and the Quebec labour minister." The editorial added that "In the end, public safety from these fanatics can only be won by smashing the FLQ with tough and thorough police work. And the chances of accomplishing that would not, so far as we can see, be improved by sacrificing Mr. Cross and Mr. Laporte." (Toronto *Daily Star*, October 12, 1970.)

8. I encountered this argument repeatedly in private discussion with supporters of government policy.

9. His mother testified to this effect at the Laporte inquest in November. (Toronto *Globe and Mail*, November 9, 1970.)

10. One member of Parliament told me on Sunday, October 11, that he welcomed a half-hour talk on the subject of the kidnapping that day because it was the first occasion he had had to apply himself to the subject. Too many other events had occurred during the week in Ottawa, including the reassembly of Parliament, the end of a session, and the formal opening of a new one, for members to give time to considering the Cross affair at length. The timing of the offence, whether accidental or not, contributed, like the choice of a victim, to the relative lack of concern applied to it in these first few days. Prime Minister Trudeau told Tom Buckley of the *New York Times* that the decision by the federal cabinet to take extraordinary measures was made without a great struggle, either "emotionally or intellectually." (See "The Testing of Pierre Trudeau," *New York Times Magazine*, December 6, 1970.)

11. See the Toronto *Globe and Mail*, October 12, 1970; Toronto *Daily Star*, October 12, 1970; *Le Devoir*, 12 octobre, 1970.

12. *Le nouvel observateur*, 22 février, 1971, p. 22.

13. Toronto *Daily Star*, October 12, 1970; *Le Devoir*, 30 octobre, 1970; Toronto *Globe and Mail*, October 31, 1970.

14. Quoted in the Toronto *Daily Star*, October 12, 1970.

15. Quoted in the Toronto *Daily Star*, October 12, 1970. See also the original text in *Le Devoir*, 13 octobre, 1970. In his book *Quebec in Question* (James Lewis and Samuel, Toronto, 1971) Marcel Rioux translates the key word "un préalable" as "a preliminary arrangement" rather than as "a prerequisite"; and he translates "la contrepartie" as "the other half of the agreement" rather than as "the counterpart." (p. 171) The sense remains the same.

16. Toronto *Daily Star*, October 13, 1970; Anthony Westell, Toronto *Daily Star*, January 16, 1971; Gérard Pelletier, *La Crise d'Octobre*, pp. 105-117.

17. *Le Devoir*, 13 octobre, 1970.

18. Toronto *Daily Star*, October 12, October 13, 1970.

19. Toronto *Daily Star*, October 13, 1970.

20. *ibid.*

21. Toronto *Daily Star*, October 12, 1970. Mr. Cross, after his release, confirmed that his messages had been dictated to him. This simply underlines the interpretation offered here of the meaning of this reply, and of Mr. Laporte's.

22. Toronto *Daily Star*, October 13, 1970.

23. Toronto *Daily Star*, October 13, 1970.

24. Robert Lemieux, who had acted for many of the FLQ terrorists previously convicted or awaiting trial, took it upon himself to act as public spokesman for the kidnappers during the week of the Cross kidnapping by interpreting each new communiqué to press correspondents. He was then named by the Liberation cell as one of three persons it wished to accompany the prisoners and their families in the event of an exchange. By the end of the week his press conferences had become fixtures in the crisis, and his face appeared as fre-

quently as anyone's on television news. No doubt his access to the
media annoyed political leaders who were less forward in the affair.
On Sunday, October 11, he was picked up by Montreal police in his
hotel room and jailed on a charge of obstructing justice; this meant
that the first meeting between Demers and Lemieux had to take
place in Lemieux's jail cell on Monday night. Justice Minister Choquette announced on Tuesday that he agreed to Lemieux's release on
his own recognizance, and following a court appearance that morning he went free on remand. (Toronto *Daily Star*, October 13, 1970.)
This clumsy bit of byplay offered comic relief in the bizarre affair.
(The charge of obstructing justice was later dismissed by the court.)

25. James Eayrs, among others, commented harshly on the absence of reassurance to the public in *Saturday Night*, April, 1971.

26. Toronto *Daily Star*, October 19, 1970. The answers to other
questions in the survey demonstrated the degree of public confusion.
Majorities also supported the view that the maintenance of law and
order was more important than saving two lives, supported the decision to broadcast the FLQ manifesto, and supported the imposition
of War Measures.

27. *Le Devoir*, 13 octobre, 1970.

28. *ibid.*

29. Toronto *Daily Star*, October 14, 1970.

30. *ibid.*

31. See the account in Ron Haggart and Aubrey E. Golden, *Rumours of War*, chapter 10, pp. 171-187.

32. *Le Devoir*, 30 octobre, 1970; translated in the *Globe and Mail*,
October 31, 1970.

33. Saulnier favoured the immediate imposition of War Measures.

34. Toronto *Globe and Mail*, October 31, 1970.

35. Coalitions were, after all, the means taken by British governments in 1916 and 1940, and by a Canadian government in 1917, to
strengthen themselves in unusual conditions of crisis.

36. Guy Joron, a Parti Québecois member of the Quebec National Assembly, recounted these assurances in a public meeting in Toronto in November, 1970.

37. This view was reflected in the statement of the "Sixteen" which is commented upon later in this chapter.

38. Prime Minister Trudeau, in a radio interview on November 3, said that Premier Bourassa had requested War Measures on October 11, but that he had restrained him for five days. (Peterborough *Examiner*, November 4, 1970.) As noted previously, Claude Ryan testifies that Lucien Saulnier favoured the adoption of War Measures that day. (Toronto *Globe and Mail*, October 31, 1970.)

39. CBC News, October 12, 1970.

40. Toronto *Globe and Mail*, October 15, 1970.

41. The text of this interview, which was severely cut by the CBC for showing on news broadcasts on October 13, is transcribed in full in the Toronto *Daily Star*, October 14, 1970.

42. Toronto *Daily Star*, October 14, 1970.

43. Toronto *Daily Star*, October 15, 1970.

44. Toronto *Globe and Mail*, October 31, 1970; Haggart and Golden, *op. cit.*, p. 19.

45. Toronto *Daily Star*, October 15, 1970.

46. Toronto *Daily Star*, October 15, 1970. The signators of the statement were:

René Lévesque, president of the Parti Québecois;
Alfred Rouleau, president of the Desjardins Life Insurance Company;
Marcel Pépin, president of the CSN (Fédération canadienne des employés de services publics, Canadian federation of government employees);
Louis Laberge, president of the FTQ (Fédération des Travailleurs du Québec, Quebec Federation of Labour);
Jean-Marc Kirouac, president of the UCC (Union Catholique des Cultivateurs, Catholic Farmers' Union);

Claude Ryan, editor of *Le Devoir*;

Jacques Parizeau, president of the executive committee of the Parti Québecois;

Yvon Charbonneau, president of the CEQ (Corporation des Enseignants du Québec, Quebec Teachers' Corporation);

Mathias Rioux, president of the Alliance des professeurs de Montréal, Montreal Teachers' Association;

Camille Laurin, parliamentary leader of the Parti Québecois;

Guy Rocher, professor of sociology at the University of Montreal;

Fernand Dumont, director of the Institut supérieur des sciences humaines (Institute of Humanities) at Laval University;

Paul Bélanger, professor of political science at Laval University;

Raymond Laliberté, ex-president of the CEQ;

Marcel Rioux, professor of sociology at the University of Montreal.

(See Marcel Rioux, *Quebec in Question*, pp. 173-174.)

47. See the further comments on this possibility in chapter 4. Gérard Pelletier makes much of this possibility in his book.

CHAPTER THREE

1. House of Commons *Debates*, October 16, 1970, p. 193.

2. The amended War Measures Act provided that a proclamation of War Measures could be revoked by resolution of both houses of Parliament introduced any time within ten days of the tabling of the proclamation. (8-9 Eliz. II C. 44.) The government's resolution was adopted by a vote of 190 to 16. All sixteen opponents were members of the New Democratic Party. The government resolution was supported by members of the Progressive Conservative and Creditiste parties. Later, in November, on second reading of the act to replace War Measures, the Public Order (Temporary Measures) Act, the government was supported by all parties; a single vote was recorded against second reading by David MacDonald (P.C., Egmont). On third reading members of the New Democratic Party joined him in opposition.

3. Revised Statues of Canada, ch. 288.

4. *ibid.*

5. House of Commons *Debates*, October 16, 1970, Appendix, p. 245.

6. *ibid.*

7. House of Commons *Debates*, October 16, 1970, p. 193; Toronto *Daily Star*, October 16, 1970.

8. Robert Lemieux sought release under habeas corpus on the ground that no state of insurrection existed and that the government therefore had no authority to proclaim the War Measures Act, but the Montreal court refused the claim on this ground.

9. The text of the Regulations appears in the Toronto *Globe and Mail*, October 17, 1970.

10. House of Commons *Debates*, October 16, October 17, 1970.

11. House of Commons *Debates*, October 23, 1970, pp. 510-511.

12. House of Commons *Debates*, October 23, 1970, p. 511.

13. House of Commons *Debates*, October 23, 1970, p. 511.

14. The question of evidence is significant because of some of the assertions about the state of anticipated insurrection made by Jean Marchand, Bryce Mackasey, Robert Bourassa, and Jean Drapeau, which will be considered later. In addition, Robert Stanfield justified his party's support for the War Measures resolution on the ground that the public evidence was incomplete, and that the benefit of the doubt in such circumstances had to be granted to the government. Mr. Stanfield stuck to this agnostic position even after the declarations of October 23 by the prime minister, and thus contributed to, or went along with, the general inclination to take the government's word for granted in the crisis, in spite of the prime minister's implied invitation to judge the action conclusively on the evidence available.

15. House of Commons *Debates*, October 16, 1970, p. 193.

16. *ibid.*

17. House of Commons *Debates*, October 16, 1970, pp. 245, 246.

18. House of Commons *Debates*, October 16, 1970, p. 194.

19. House of Commons *Debates*, October 16, 1970, p. 211.

20. *ibid.*

21. House of Commons *Debates*, October 16, 1970, p. 212.

22. House of Commons *Debates*, November 4, 1970, p. 879.

23. As James Eayrs pointed out with acerbity, the justice minister in his eagerness to seek support for his case mistakenly identified Justice Sanford as "Chief Justice," and falsely claimed that his opinion had been shared by Justice Oliver Wendell Holmes. Holmes had, in fact, dissented from the judgment in unusually strong language. Eayrs concluded: " . . . have we not a right to expect that our public philosophers, for all their shallowness and inexperience, will refrain from distorting the wisdom of the classics to bolster their case? However urgently that case may be in need of reinforcement?" ("Did John Turner have his quotes right?," Toronto *Daily Star*, November 17, 1970.)

24. CBC Television News, October 16, 1970.

25. Peter Newman reported that this information came from "a secret document that clearly outlined the scenario of the FLQ revolt," which was in the hands of Mr. Trudeau and Mr. Bourassa. (Toronto *Daily Star*, October 30, 1970.) Much later, in January, 1971, Tom Hazlitt of the Toronto *Daily Star* referred to "a secret communiqué" from the FLQ whose existence has "never been officially confirmed" which, he says, "was probably the factor that tipped the scales in favour of imposition of the War Measures Act." The FLQ, he suggests, threatened "more kidnappings, indiscriminate killing of politicians and police officers, and a series of power line bombings that would have reduced Montreal to a city of darkness and fear. This suppressed document gave police the bargaining power they needed to convince Premier Robert Bourassa and indirectly Prime Minister Pierre Trudeau that something approaching a state of 'apprehended insurrection' existed in Quebec . . . (Toronto *Daily Star*, January 16, 1971.) Another document, seized in 1969 during the anti terrorist squad's raids on Company of Young Canadians offices in Montreal, and titled "Revolutionary Strategy and the Role of the Avant-Garde," outlined a three-phase struggle in less detail, omitting mention of kidnapping and selective assassination. This pamphlet had been in Otta-

wa's possession, along with other seditious materials, since the November, 1969, parliamentary investigation of the Montreal section of the Company of Young Canadians. In addition, the CBC had recently broadcast a television interview with two members of the FLQ training with the Palestinian guerrillas, in which they mentioned that the next step in the FLQ program would be "selective assassination." Suddenly this kind of bravado was taken seriously.

26. See Peter C. Newman, "Why Trudeau pounced: Quebec was on verge of a 'classic' revolt," Toronto *Daily Star*, October 30, 1970; Haggart and Golden, *op. cit.*, p. 176.

27. Toronto *Daily Star*, October 30, 1970.

28. In an interview with Tom Gould on CFTO-TV and the CTV network, December 31, 1970.

29. Toronto *Daily Star*, October 30, 1970. This article, to which several references are made in the previous paragraph, appears to depend upon official sources for its information. Given Mr. Newman's confidential sources in Ottawa, and given that the article reflects so precisely most aspects of the official case as it was stated elsewhere, the article itself takes on a semi-official appearance. Another article of the same kind, reviewing Ottawa's case for War Measures on the basis of further official leaks, is Anthony Westell's "War Measures Act was invoked to restore the public's confidence" (Toronto *Daily Star*, January 16, 1971). Westell makes his own critical comments, but the body of the article depends upon official information, including what Mr. Westell refers to as "a confidential log of day-to-day developments during the crisis. . . . completed in the East Block by executive officers."

30. The *Shorter Oxford English Dictionary* defines insurrection as "the action of rising in arms or open resistance against established authority or governmental restraint . . . an armed rising, a revolt; an incipient or limited rebellion."

31. *Le Devoir* reported deep division in the Bourassa cabinet over the question of negotiations, as mentioned earlier in chapter 2.

32. Quoted in the Toronto *Daily Star*, October 17, 1970.

33. The clearest exposition of Mr. Trudean's view that the public

should "stand up and be counted," and that drawing this kind of sharp line in the crisis would strengthen the federalist position in Quebec in the long run, was made by the prime minister in an interview on the CBC television program "Encounter" on November 5, 1970.

34. House of Commons *Debates*, November 4, 1970, p. 881.

35. See especially Jean Marchand's speech in the House on War Measures, House of Commons *Debates*, October 16, 1970, pp. 222-225.

36. As previously noted, the text was reprinted in the Toronto *Daily Star*, October 17, 1970.

37. See the report in the Toronto *Daily Star*, January 6, 1971.

38. Quoted in *Scanlan's Magazine*, January, 1971, p. 67.

39. Toronto *Globe and Mail*, December 10, 1970.

40. Quoted in the Toronto *Daily Star*, January 5, 1971.

41. Pierre Vallières, *White Niggers of America* (McClelland and Stewart, Toronto, 1971), p. 228.

42. Quoted in the Toronto *Daily Star*, November 9, 1970.

43. See above, page 10

44. See above, page 26

CHAPTER FOUR

1. See George Woodcock, "Anarchism and Violence," *Canadian Forum*, January, 1971, p. 335; Pierre Vallières, *White Niggers of America*, p. 258.

2. As George Woodcock points out in the Prologue to his *Anarchism* (Meridian Books, New York, 1962), it is wrong to identify anarchism necessarily with terrorism, and I do not intend to do so here. But it is particularly the terrorist element in nineteenth century anarchism which seems to have parallels in Quebec today, and it is that element which I am concerned with in this chapter. Woodcock notes that:

Anarchists may be substantially agreed on their ultimate general aims; on the tactics needed to reach that aim they have shown singular disagreement, and this is particularly the case with regard to violence. The Tolstoyans admitted violence under no circumstances; Godwin sought to bring change through discussion and Proudhon and his followers through the peaceful proliferation of cooperative organizations; Kropotkin accepted violence, but only reluctantly and because he felt it occurred inevitably during revolutions and that revolutions were unavoidable stages in human progress; even Bakunin, though he fought on many barricades and extolled the bloodthirstiness of peasant risings, had also times of doubt. . . .

In fact, where anarchists did accept violence it was largely because of their adherence to traditions that stem from the French, American, and ultimately the English revolutions—traditions of violent popular action in the name of liberty which they shared with other movements of their time such as the Jacobins, the Marxists, the Blanquists, and the followers of Mazzini and Garibaldi. . . . There were, indeed, special situations, particularly in Spain, Italy, and Russia, where violence had long been endemic in political life, and here the anarchists, like other parties, accepted insurrectionism almost as routine; but among the celebrities of anarchist history the heroes of violent action have been far outnumbered by the paladins of the word. (pp. 15-16)

3. James Joll, *The Anarchists* (London, Eyre & Spottiswoode, 1964), p. 12.

4. I am grateful to Professor Stuart Robson for emphasizing this point of comparison.

5. See Charles Taylor, "Behind the Kidnappings: Alienation too Profound for the System to Contain," *Canadian Dimension*, December, 1970, pp. 26-29.

6. Irving Kristol, "'When virtue loses all her loveliness'–some reflections on capitalism and 'the free society,'" in *The Public Interest*, Number 21, Fall, 1970, p. 3.

7. Gerald Brenan, *The Spanish Labyrinth* (Cambridge University Press, 1962), p. 162.

8. Brenan, p. 136. There is a distinction of both experience and

purpose between the earlier, nostalgic and rural anarchism of, say, Proudhon, and the urban anarchism of the turn of the century. As Stuart Robson writes, the West European anarchists of that period can "best be seen as examples of the proletarianization of the newly educated, as 'outsiders' whose education had left them irrelevant to the increasingly organized society of Western Europe. Whatever their parents did for a living, and whatever their own early careers, they pass through the watershed of education and nothing is waiting for them afterwards." The contemporary parallel in Quebec is obvious and unsettling.

9. Quoted in Joll, *op. cit.*, p. 110.

10. Joll, p. 111.

11. Although after the event, Gérard Pelletier granted in his book, *La Crise d'Octobre*, that this was not an objective of the FLQ. It is difficult to determine from his account what his assessment was at that time, or whether, if it was consistent with his later judgment, it had any influence upon the federal cabinet's decision. (See *La Crise d'Octobre*, p. 59.)

12. The document is reproduced in the Montreal Star's pamphlet, *The FLQ: Seven Years of Terrorism*, p. 10.

13. This document also appears, in part, in *The FLQ: Seven Years of Terrorism*, p. 50; in Gérard Pelletier's *La Crise d'Octobre* (Appendice II, pp. 237-240); and in full in *Our Generation* (Volume 7, Number 3, October-November, 1970) pp. 69-75. The attorney for the City of Montreal, Michel Côté, attributed the pamphlet to Pierre Vallières. (See Haggart and Golden, *op. cit.*, p. 165.)

14. Vallières, *op. cit.*, pp. 222-223.

15. See also *The FLQ: Seven Years of Terrorism*, p. 80.

16. Quoted in Brenan, *op. cit.*, p. 143.

17. "The deeply moralistic element in anarchism, which makes it much more than a mere political doctrine, has never been explored adequately, and this is due partly to the reluctance of the anarchists themselves, who have rejected conventional moralities, to stress this aspect of their own philosophy. Nevertheless, the urge to simplicity is part of an ascetic attitude which permeates anarchist thought. The

anarchist does not merely feel anger against the wealthy; he feels anger against wealth itself, and in his eyes the rich man is as much a victim of his luxury as the poor man of his destitution. To enable all men to live in luxury, that vision which bedevils North American democracy, has never appealed to the anarchists." (George Woodcock, *op. cit.*, p. 28.)

18. Vallières, *op. cit.*, p. 253.

19. Pelletier, *op. cit.*, p. 57. (Translation mine)

20. This was true in a number of cases at the turn of the century. But it is an incomplete account of the disasters of anarchist terrorism, because one anarchist act, in 1914–the murder at Sarajevo–was the occasion for the slide into the First World War. In Sorel's terms, the war could be seen as the unexpected fulfillment of the anarchist dream of social collapse before the millenium. Fascist and Nazi disciples of Sorel took up that apocalyptic faith after the war. But this terrible aberration does not, I think, weaken the notion of a general cyclical pattern of terrorist activity when it operates in isolation from larger events.

21. See, for example, Gerald Brenan, *op. cit.*, pp. 163-164; Barbara Tuchman, *The Proud Tower* (Macmillan, New York, 1966), p. 77. Robert Lemieux asserted on October 8, 1970, that the Cross kidnapping was motivated by the failings of the judicial apparatus and the administration of justice in Canada. (*Le Devoir*, 9 octobre, 1970.)

22. Brenan, *op. cit.*, p. 146.

23. Ann Charney, "From Redpath Crescent to Rue des Recollets," *Canadian Forum*, January, 1971, pp. 325-326.

24. Quoted in *Scanlan's*, January, 1971, p. 68.

25. Vallières, *op. cit.*, p. 261.

26. A story in the Toronto *Daily Star* on December 4, 1970, quoted a resident of a nearby house who knew two of the kidnappers by sight as commenting on their public movements, "Well, you should know this area is strongly separatist."

27. Vallières, *op. cit.*, pp. 213-214.

28. Brenan, *op. cit.*, p. 154.

29. Barbara Tuchman, *op. cit.*, p. 88.

30. See the report by Tom Hazlitt in the Toronto *Daily Star*, January 16, 1971.

31. Private information.

32. On the state of nerves in Montreal and its results, see the *Globe and Mail*, October 13, 1970; *Globe and Mail*, October 21, 1970. See also the reference in Jean-Claude Trait, *FLQ 70: Offensive d'automne* (Les éditions de l'homme, Montreal, 1970), p. 119.

33. House of Commons *Debates*, October 16, 1970, pp. 222-225.

34. A.R.M. Lower, *Colony to Nation* (Toronto, Longmans, Green and Co., Third edition, 1957), p. 499.

35. J. Bartlett Brebner, *Canada: A Modern History* (Ann Arbor, The University of Michigan Press, New edition, 1970), pp. 495-496.

36. House of Commons *Debates*, July 1, 1960, p. 5651.

37. Quoted in *Scanlan's*, January, 1971, p. 67.

38. Quoted in Marcel Rioux, *Quebec in Question*, pp. 172-173.

CHAPTER FIVE

1. Quoted in Rioux, *Quebec in Question*, p. 170. The address also appears in full, as previously noted, in *Le Devoir*, 13 octobre, 1970, and the Toronto *Daily Star*, October 12, 1970.

2. He expressed his views in an interview on CBC Television News, October 16, 1970.

3. Quoted in Toronto *Daily Star*, October 14, 1970.

4. Haggart and Golden, *op. cit.*, p. 257.

5. Quoted in *Liberal* (Liberal Party in Ontario and Liberal Federation of Canada, Extra Post Convention Issue, March, 1971).

6. This is made clear at many points in his writings, and particular-

ly in his essays on popular sovereignty written for the Quebec public in 1958 and recently published in English as *Approaches to Politics* (Oxford University Press, Toronto, 1970).

7. Toronto *Daily Star*, October 17, 1970.

8. *Approaches to Politics*, p. 87.

9. Marchand's and Drapeau's statements about FRAP are reported in *Le Devoir*, 22 octobre and 23 octobre, 1970. Dr. Henri Bellemarre and Jean Roy were the two prominent FRAP candidates who were detained. (Roy was also the printer for FRAP.) A third candidate, André Gravel, was also detained and released without charge. (See Serge Mongeau, M.D., *Kidnappé par la police* (Editions du jour, Montreal, 1970), pp. 119-128. The request to postpone the civic election was made by *Le Devoir* in an editorial on October 23, 1970, and by the Parti Québecois, as reported in *Le Devoir* on the same day.

10. In the campaign for the mayoralty, which FRAP did not contest, Mr. Drapeau received ninety-two percent of the popular vote. In the contests for council seats, the Civic Party won all seats with an average of eighty percent of the vote. (Toronto *Daily Star*, October 26, 1970.)

11. For example, when the National Policy Conference of the Liberal Federation of Canada voted 492 to 424 favouring the amendment of the Public Order Act (then under debate in Parliament) to create a federal supervisory commission which would oversee Quebec's use of emergency powers under the Act, the federal cabinet rejected the recommendation. Peter Reilly gives this account of the attitude of Marc Lalonde, the prime minister's special assistant:

> At the Liberal policy conference in Harrison Hot Springs last November, his concept of participatory democracy was made stunningly plain when he was asked during a workshop meeting about the value, to the P.M.'s office, of resolutions passed by riding associations. He made it clear that he was not impressed by such statements of local feeling, explaining that "people in riding associations don't have the sophisticated knowledge and information required. They're uninformed."
>
> "Suppose," he went on, "that the riding association in Burnaby had a meeting and somebody got up and said 'wouldn't it be a great idea to stop all defence spending?' Would you expect

it to immediately become government policy? Of course not, it's silly." But, he was asked, what if fifty-one percent of all Liberal party members in Canada wanted to eliminate defence spending? Would that have a chance of becoming government policy?

"No, not even if seventy-five percent wanted it, it doesn't mean the government would."

Well then, his questioners went on, precisely how would the government view such an occurrence? *The government would conclude*, Lalonde said, *that its defence policy was not being understood, and that some cabinet ministers had better get out and do a better selling job.* Mercifully, the matter was allowed to drop there, but even in its incompleteness, the incident provides a valuable key to understanding this government. (*Saturday Night*, October, 1970, p. 22)

12. For an account of these events in detail, see Patrick Seale and Maureen McConville, *French Revolution 1968* (Penguin Books, London, 1968), *passim*, and especially chapter 14, pp. 189-206.

13. There was, to be sure, a strong Hobbesian element in the President's calculation. Before announcing his decision to hold onto office, de Gaulle visited a French army garrison in West Germany to assure himself of their willingness to defend his claim to authority, and armoured units were moved to the outskirts of Paris as a result. (See Seale and McConville, *op. cit.*, pp. 203-205.)

14. Jacques Maritain, *Man and the State* (University of Chicago Press, 1951), p. 139.

15. *ibid.*, p. 140.

16. *ibid.*, p. 141.

17. *ibid.*, p. 141.

18. *ibid.*, p. 141.

19. *ibid.*, p. 142.

20. *ibid.*, p. 143.

21. *ibid.*, p. 145.

22. *ibid.*, p. 145.

23. *ibid.*, p. 145.

24. *ibid.*, p. 146.

CHAPTER SIX

1. Pierre Elliott Trudeau, *Federalism and the French Canadians* (Macmillan, Toronto, 1968), Foreword, p. xix. This is henceforth referred to as *Federalism*.

2. The first part of this tale of conversion is recounted in Donald Peacock's *Journey to Power: The Story of a Canadian Election* (Ryerson Press, Toronto, 1968), chapters 5-12, pp. 124-383; and in Peter C. Newman's *The Distemper of Our Times* (McClelland and Stewart, Toronto, 1968), pp. 316-332 and 435-469.

3. John T. Saywell, in the Introduction to *Federalism*, p. vii.

4. In the Preface to *Federalism*, p. xvi.

5. *Federalism*, Foreword, pp. xxi, xxii.

6. A number of books dealing with the leadership conventions of 1967 and 1968, and the 1968 general election, made descriptive reference to Mr. Trudeau's thought. Among academic commentators, Ramsay Cook has been most thorough and prolific, though admiring and uncritical. See, for example, his Introduction to *Approaches to Politics*, and his essay, "Federalism, Nationalism and the Canadian Nation-State," in *The Maple Leaf Forever* (Macmillan, Toronto, 1971), pp. 23-45. One perceptive critic has been Gad Horowitz, in his "Trudeau vs Trudeauism," *The Canadian Forum*, May, 1968, pp. 29, 30.

7. Quoted in Tom Buckley, "The Testing of Pierre Trudeau," *New York Times Magazine*, December 6, 1971, pp. 146, 148.

8. The most important of these were: "La province de Québec au moment de la grève," in *La Grève de l'amiante* (P. E. Trudeau, ed., Editions Cité Libre, Montreal, 1956, and Editions du jour, Montreal, 1970); "Some Obstacles to Democracy in Quebec," in the *Canadian Journal of Economics and Political Science* (Vol. XXIV, No. 3, August, 1958); "The Practice and Theory of Federalism" in *Social Purpose for Canada* (Michael Oliver, ed., University of Toronto Press, 1961); "La nouvelle trahison des clercs," in *Cité Libre* (April, 1962); "Separatist

Counter-Revolutionaries." in *Cité Libre* (May, 1964); "Federalism, Nationalism and Reason," in *The Future of Canadian Federalism* (P.-A. Crépeau and C. B. Macpherson eds., University of Toronto Press, 1965); and "Quebec and the Constitutional Problem," a paper prepared in 1965. The first essay appears in part in translation as "Quebec on the Eve of the Asbestos Strike," in Ramsay Cook, ed., *French-Canadian Nationalism: An Anthology* (Macmillan of Canada, Toronto, 1969); the other six are reprinted in Pierre Elliott Trudeau, *Federalism and the French Canadians* (Macmillan of Canada, Toronto, 1968).

9. *Federalism*, p. 8.

10. *ibid.*, p. 11.

11. *ibid.*, p. 11.

12. *ibid.*, pp. 11, 12.

13. *ibid.*, p. 13.

14. *ibid.*, p. 15.

15. *ibid.*, p. 15.

16. *ibid.*, p. 15.

17. The paper was prepared as background for a submission by some Quebec labour and agricultural organizations to the Constitution Committee of the Quebec Legislative Assembly in 1965.

18. *Federalism*, p. 22.

19. *ibid.*, p. 156.

20. *ibid.*, p. 157.

21. *ibid.*, pp. 161-167.

22. *ibid.*, pp. 167-168.

23. *ibid.*, p. 168.

24. *ibid.*, pp. 168-169.

25. *ibid.*, p. 169.

26. *ibid.*, p. 210.

27. *ibid.*, p. 211.

28. *ibid.*, p. 206.

29. *ibid.*, p. 206.

30. *ibid.*, p. 170.

31. *ibid.*, p. 164.

32. *ibid.*, p. 200.

33. *ibid.*, p. 165.

34. *ibid.*, pp. 166-167.

35. *ibid.*, p. 177.

36. *ibid.*, p. 159.

37. *ibid.*, p. 202.

38. *ibid.*, p. 203.

39. *ibid.*, p. 154.

40. *ibid.*, p. 27.

41. Both sets of reforming proposals are advocated in "Quebec and the Constitutional Problem" (1965) and "A Constitutional Declaration of Rights" (1967).

42. *Federalism*, pp. 48-49.

43. *ibid.*, p. 49.

44. See the article by F. G. Vallee and N. Shulman, "The viability of French groupings outside Quebec," in Mason Wade, ed., *Regionalism in the Canadian Community 1867-1967* (University of Toronto Press, 1969), pp. 83-99.

45. See, *inter alia*, "Some Obstacles to Democracy in Quebec," in *Federalism*, especially p. 112.

46. *Federalism*, pp. 56, 58.

47. *A Preliminary Report of the Royal Commission on Bilingualism and Biculturalism* (Ottawa, Queen's Printer, 1965), p. 13.

48. See *The Confederation of Tomorrow Conference, Proceedings* and *Theme Papers* (Queen's Printer, Toronto, 1967).

49. *Report of the Royal Commission on Bilingualism and Biculturalism*, Book I (Ottawa, Queen's Printer, 1967), Preface, p. xviii.

50. Their letter is reproduced in *Le Devoir*, 19 mars, 1971.

51. *Le Devoir*, 19 mars, 1971.

52. *Le Devoir*, 19 mars, 1971.

53. See especially his comments in "Some Obstacles to Democracy in Quebec," in *Federalism*, pp. 118-120.

54. *ibid.*, p. 119.

55. George Grant, "Nationalism and rationality," *Canadian Forum*, January, 1971, p. 336.

CHAPTER SEVEN

1. Vallières, *op. cit.*, p. 204.

2. *ibid.*, p. 205.

3. *ibid.*, p. 206.

4. See *La Crise d'Octobre*, pp. 197-213. Gad Horowitz examines the nature of this "complacency" in a review of Pelletier's book, "Les perils de la complaisance," *Le Devoir*, 10 avril, 1971.

5. Toronto *Globe and Mail*, April 30, 1970.

6. *Le Devoir*, 9 février, 1971. Though Chambly was overshadowed by the constitutional conference then in progress, it was regarded by the Parti Québecois as a highly significant result. Four things were working for the Quebec government in the by-election: a crisis in which the distinction between democratic and revolutionary separatism had been blurred; the emotional significance of Chambly being Pierre Laporte's seat; the fact that the government candidate was already a cabinet minister; and the fact, too, that he was a former

Union Nationale minister who might expect to carry some U.N. support with him. Nevertheless the P.Q. not only maintained but increased its share of the vote, in the face of a very high turnout of English-speaking voters who could be expected to support the government virtually unanimously.

7. See the analysis of the vote in Vincent Lemieux, Marcel Gilbert, André Blais, *Une élection de réalignment* (Editions du jour, Montreal, 1970).

8. For a critical comment on this interpretation of the result, see the editorial in the *Journal of Canadian Studies*, May, 1970.

9. The fundamental importance of this threat as a motivating force behind the Parti Québecois is made clear in René Lévesque's *An Option for Quebec* (McClelland and Stewart, Toronto, 1968) and in Marcel Rioux's *Quebec in Question*.

10. See "Some Obstacles to Democracy in Quebec," *Federalism*, pp. 103-123.

11. "Utopia is always a picture and a measure of the moral heights man could attain using only his natural powers, 'purely by the natural light'. . . . It is a vision not of the probable but of the 'not-impossible.' It is not concerned with the historically likely at all. Utopia is nowhere, not only geographically, but historically as well. It exists neither in the past nor in the future. Indeed, its esthetic and intellectual tension arises precisely from the melancholy contrast between what might be and what will be. . . . It is a perfection that the mind's eye recognizes as true and which is described as such, and so serves as a standard of moral judgment." (Judith Shklar, "The political theory of utopia: from melancholy to nostalgia," in Frank E. Manuel, ed., *Utopias and Utopian Thought* (Beacon Paperbacks, 1967), pp. 104-105.

12. In his interview with Tom Buckley of the *New York Times* he said: "I've written often enough that the country is held together only by consent, not by force of arms. If any part of our country wants to leave Canada I don't think force of arms will be used to prevent it.

You can't hold a modern nation together by force. You have to hold it together by showing the people that their lot, their future, their destiny is better within the country than without . . . if a whole province decides that it is happier outside the country, then it will leave." (*New York Times Magazine*, December 6, 1970.)

13. *Canadian Forum*, January, 1971, p. 337.

14. The *New Yorker*, April 10, 1971, p. 30.

15. The speculation that follows is entirely my own and owes nothing to consultation with any Quebec politician or public figure. (I would not want to be accused of plotting the formation of a provisional government.)

Works cited

The author and publisher acknowledge with thanks the following individuals and publishers who have granted permission to quote from the works indicated: *Daedalus*, Journal of the American Academy of Arts and Sciences, Boston, Massachusetts (for quotation from Judith Shklar's article, "The Political Theory of Utopia: From Melancholy to Nostalgia," *Daedalus*, Vol. 94, Number 2 [Spring 1965]); Cambridge University Press, American Branch (for quotation from Gerald Brenan, *The Spanish Labyrinth*); Ann Charney (for quotation from an article in *The Canadian Forum*, January, 1971); The University of Chicago Press (for quotation from Jacques Maritain, *Man and the State*, © 1951 by The University of Chicago Press); Editions du jour (for quotation in translation from Gérard Pelletier, *La Crise d'Octobre*); Professor George P. Grant (for quotation from an article in *The Canadian Forum*, January, 1971); James Lewis and Samuel, Publishers (for quotation from Marcel Rioux, *Quebec in Question*); James Joll (for quotation from his book *The Anarchists*); Irving Kristol and *The Public Interest* (for quotation from an article in *The Public Interest*, Number 21, Fall, 1970, © 1970 by National Affairs, Inc.); Longman Canada Limited (for quotation from A.R.M. Lower, *Colony to Nation*); The Macmillan Company, New York (for quotation from Barbara Tuchman, *The Proud Tower*); The Macmillan Company of Canada Limited (for quotation from Pierre Elliott

Trudeau, *Federalism and the French Canadians*); Mrs. Patricia Claxton (for quotation from her English translation of Pierre Elliott Trudeau's "New Treason of the Intellectuals" in *Federalism and the French Canadians*); The Canadian Publishers, McClelland and Stewart Limited, Toronto (for quotation from Pierre Vallières, *White Niggers of America*); The World Publishing Company (for quotation from George Woodcock's *Anarchism*, © 1962 by Meridian Books, Inc.); new press (for quotation from Ron Haggart and Aubrey E. Golden, *Rumours of War*); Oxford University Press (for quotation from Pierre Eliott Trudeau, *Approaches to Politics*, translated by I. M. Owen, © Oxford University Press [Canadian Branch] 1970); Peter Reilly (for quotation from an article in *Saturday Night*, October, 1970); University of Toronto Press (for quotation from Pierre Elliott Trudeau, "Federalism, Nationalism and Reason," in P.-A. Crépeau and C. B. Macpherson, editors, *The Future of Canadian Federalism*).